WOMEN AND INDUSTRIALISATION

WOMEN
AND
INDUSTRIALISATION

By

Dr. M. Lakshmi Narasaiah
M.A., Ph.D.

Professor of Economics
Co-ordinator, Dept. of M.B.A. and Commerce
Special Officer
Sri Krishnadevaraya University Post-graduate Centre
Kurnool–518 002
Andhra Pradesh
(India)

DISCOVERY PUBLISHING HOUSE
NEW DELHI-110002

First Published-2007

ISBN 81-8356-237-X

Published by

DISCOVERY PUBLISHING HOUSE
4831/24, Ansari Road, Prahlad Street,
Darya Ganj, New Delhi-110002 (India)
Phone: 23279245 • Fax: 91-11-23253475
E-mail: dphbooks@rediffmail.com
dphtemp@indiatimes.com

Printed at:

Sachin Printers, Delhi

Preface

Not only do women in India suffer greater poverty than men, they often have little choice but to pass it on to the next generation. Investing in women, therefore, is an effective way of building a better economic future for the poor.

Research findings from all sources are confirming what development practitioners have long observed: women are generally worse off economically than men, and the consequences of their poverty are more serious for future generations.

Women's poverty differs from that of men both in degree and in kind: women experience greater poverty and transmit their disadvantage more readily to their children, thus perpetuating the poverty cycle. At the same time, however, they are better able than men to protect children from the consequences of poverty.

It is this close connection between women's and children's fortunes that makes women's poverty a prime target for enlightened development practice. Anti-poverty policies need to reach poor women both to maximise social return on development investments and minimise the poverty of this and the next generation.

Breaking the Poverty Cycle

Poor women's rising participation in the world of paid work, however, does not necessarily guarantee a destiny of poverty. On the contrary, their earnings can protect children from poverty. Until fairly recently, the prevailing assumption was that any positive income effect of women's employment on children's health and well-being would be offset by negative effects of reduced childcare time by working mothers or by the substitution of older siblings in childcare. Recent studies, however, indicate a positive effect of women's employment on child health and nutrition. Women prefer to invest meagre earnings on child well-being and underscore the point that the income poor women earn can yield higher social benefits than income earned by men.

These positive effects of poor women's income-earning activities are not necessarily contradictory with the negative effects of women's increased work on their daughter's educational opportunities. It is likely that women need a minimum level of income to act on their preference to invest scarce resource on child well-being, below which their additional work perpetuates rather than halts poverty.

Policy and Research Implications

It is therefore desirable to implement policies that reinforce the virtuous cycle between women's and children's well-being that can occur in poor families when women have more income, and avoid those that can instead trigger a vicious cycle of deprivation between mothers and children. Circumstances which increase poor women's unpaid or very low-paid work can foster the perpetuation of disadvantage. These include the effects of declining household incomes during economic downturns, the decrease in service provision by the State which accompanies structural adjustment programmes, and many community and child-centered interventions that rely heavily on women's unpaid time. Anti-poverty packages need to reinforce poor women's roles as economic producers and avoid actions which increase women's unpaid labour for the promotion of family child welfare.

Dr. M. Lakshmi Narasaiah

Contents

1

Equal Opportunities for Women in the Community

Over half the people in the Indian community are women. The change in women's contribution to society is one of the most striking phenomena of the late twentieth century. But although they have had the law behind them, women have yet to enjoy the equality they are entitled to in theory. Men need to contribute more to family life, while women have yet to make a real impact on decisions affecting the lives of everybody.

Technological advances have meant the decline of employment in manufacturing, and the growing dominance of service industries. This has meant more jobs for women, but not necessarily better working conditions. Most women are still in lower-paid jobs, and most still work mainly with other women in similar jobs and fields. Women are still under-represented in many sectors of industry, the professions and public service.

More and more women are involved in paid work. There is no job they cannot do, and they are entitled to equal pay for equal work, as well as the same terms and conditions at work, and the same opportunities for promotion. Giving women the opportunity to realise their potential in all spheres of society is increasingly important, for all only by involving both sexes to the full can we develop human resources on really democratic lines.

Equal Pay, Equal Opportunities

The right to equal pay for equal work without discrimination based on sex has to be set out. Equal treatment in access to employment, training, promotion and working conditions has to be encouraged. Equal treatment in social security, as well as for the self-employed are very much needed. Rights to maternity leave and pay, and a guarantee of adequate health and safety at work for pregnant women and nursing mothers are urgent. The government has to encourage good practice on: Positive action, vocational training, childcare, combating unemployment, equal opportunities in schools, integrating women into working life, combating unwanted sexual behaviour at work, education, and updating protective legislation affecting women. There is still a great deal to be done before we can claim women in the community really get a fair deal and a chance to show what they can do.

Women are still often segregated into jobs that are less well-paid than those typically taken by men. They are often well qualified than men, and the jobs they do are often less secure. These are the kinds of inequalities the society must continue to combat and it will do so, as one of the ways of making sure women do not bear the brunt. Quality and quantity in women's employment is very important.

Better Opportunities to Earn a Living

Getting more women into paid work by promoting job opportunities, entrepreneurship and local employment should be the aim. The aim should be to help them fulfil their potential through better education, training and positive action. Upgrading their skills and equipping them with hi-tech know-how is a priority. Another major concern is helping parents juggle work and caring responsibilities via better services and terms of employment.

Getting Women in Positions of Power

It is hard to believe over half the community's

population is female, given how little direct influence women have over what happens in our society. In an electoral constituency where half the voters are women, and where concerns for education, family health and food are paramount, both contestants up for election are male, and they speak to a largely male audience. The women, who work long hours and worry and sacrifice for their families and homes, fuss with the tea, hush the children, over on the periphery. If they are there at all. Politics is 'men's business'.

Training to Keep up with the Times

Women need training if they are to benefit from growth and technological development. A network of training schemes, have to be set up to develop training for women, to publicize their needs, promote information exchanges and encourage the involvement of employers and trade unions.

Changing Minds in School

There is no job women cannot do. A working party is looking at ways of encouraging boys and girls to range more widely in the subjects they take in school. It should aim to support teachers trying to avoid reproducing anachronistic stereotypes.

Pregnant women, mothers of new-born babies and nursing mothers should have the peace of mind of knowing they have secure health and social rights. For women who already have to combine their professional life with running a home and looking after children, political activity requires considerable sacrifices. Woman would be more ready to take them on if they thought they stood a chance of recognition on a par with men. That is far from being the case. If equal opportunities for women are provided definitely the country will develop at faster rate.

❑❑❑

2

Lightening the Load for Women

Not only do women in India suffer greater poverty than men, they often have little choice but to pass it on to the next generation. Investing in women, therefore, is an effective way of building a better economic future for the poor.

Research findings from all sources are confirming what development practitioners have long observed: women are generally worse off economically than men, and the consequences of their poverty are more serious for future generations.

Women's poverty differs from that of men both in degree and in kind: women experience greater poverty and transmit their disadvantage more readily to their children, thus perpetuating the poverty cycle. At the same time, however, they are better able than men to protect children from the consequences of poverty.

It is this close connection between women's and children's fortunes that makes women's poverty a prime target for enlightened development practice. Anti-poverty policies need to reach poor women both to maximise social return on development investments and minimise the poverty of this and the next generation.

Breaking the Poverty Cycle

Poor women's rising participation in the world of paid work, however, does not necessarily guarantee a destiny of poverty. On the contrary, their earnings can protect children from poverty. Until fairly recently, the prevailing assumption was that any positive income effect of women's employment on children's health and well-being would be offset by negative effects of reduced childcare time by working mothers or by the substitution of older siblings in childcare. Recent studies, however, indicate a positive effect of women's employment on child health and nutrition. Women prefer to invest meagre earnings on child well-being and underscore the point that the income poor women earn can yield higher social benefits than income earned by men.

These positive effects of poor women's income-earning activities are not necessarily contradictory with the negative effects of women's increased work on their daughter's educational opportunities. It is likely that women need a minimum level of income to act on their preference to invest scarce resources on child well-being, below which their additional work perpetuates rather than halts poverty.

Policy and Research Implications

It is therefore desirable to implement policies that reinforce the virtuous cycle between women's and children's well-being that can occur in poor families when women have more income, and avoid those that can instead trigger a vicious cycle of deprivation between mothers and children. Circumstances which increase poor women's unpaid or very low-paid work can foster the perpetuation of disadvantage. These include the effects of declining household incomes during economic downturns, the decrease in service provision by the State which accompanies structural adjustment programmes, and many community and child-centered interventions that rely heavily on women's unpaid time. Anti-poverty packages need to reinforce poor women's roles as economic producers and avoid actions which increase women's unpaid labour for the promotion of family child welfare.

Projects which increase women's productivity in home and market production and expand their employment options can help turn the vicious cycle of poverty into a virtuous one. This necessitates executing agencies which can work with women, in budget allocations to strengthen the capacity of institutions to implement and monitor gender-responsive employment programmes for the poor.

The reach of project interventions is restricted, however. Their impact is often short-lived and while they can help to contain the cycle of poverty between mothers and children, they cannot in themselves transform women's economic activities. Changes in the policy environment are required for the latter. These include agricultural policies which target poor farmers and give women farmers access to land, credit and technical assistance; financial policies which promote the growth of small enterprises and foster entrepreneurship among women; and labour-intensive "pro-poor" economic growth policies. In addition, governments need to invest in upgrading women's occupational skills, and in a series of complementary measures, including overhauling social security systems, establishing gender-friendly regulatory frameworks for agricultural and industrial growth, and legislate on childcare options.

To guide these policies, we need research that distinguishes families from households and seeks to understand the formation, structure and dynamics of families headed by women; longitudinal studies which provide a narrative for events in women's lives and assess the transmission of disadvantage between mothers and children; trend data which tracks changes in women's work as a result of changes in economic conditions and in implementation of economic and social policies; and, analyses of the mechanics, costs and consequences of targeting interventions to female heads of households and poor women.

The policy-oriented research agenda is perhaps as ambitious as the policy agenda and both require funding.

Investing in women should be an effective use of scarce development resources if these actions are guided by the basic principle of seeing women in India for what they are economic and social agents and not merely passive recipients of welfare.

❑❑❑

3

Fighting for Equality on All Fronts

In the wake of unemployment, global competition and deregulation, more and more women are joining an unforgiving job market. Are they in a position to exercise force against the discrimination they experience, and can they impose equality of opportunity? To change things women need to enter into combat on several fronts.

"For a long time, companies considered publicity to be a luxury and, in difficult times, the 'advertising and communications' budget was always the first to be slashed. Today, employers have become more aware that publicity has become a trump card in their strategy. Why can't a similar awareness become possible on the subject of women's employment?"

Financial problems and an evolution of mentality are the two core themes discussed in this chapter on the Equality of Women in the world of work.

A Dual Observation

It is of a two-fold general observation: women are more increasingly joining the ranks of the active population: however, this trend is not matched by a parallel improvement in the quality of jobs to which they have access.

It is foreseen that women's rate of participation will be close to that of men by the year 2010. In developing countries, the rate of women's activity is only 31 per cent on average, but this figure does not take into account the very large female participation in the informal sector and in agriculture. Thus, for example, in India, the adoption of a more general definition of "economic activity" pushed the participation of women from 13 to 88 per cent.

Women remained constrained in a relatively limited number of "feminine" sectors and occupations which are generally less well-paid and are less prestigious. During the last decade, however, an upward trend has emerged and more women are acceding to management and administrative post and to specialised and technical professions. Moreover, an increasing number of women are setting up their own businesses. It can be noted, nonetheless, that very few salaried women are able to reach the higher echelons of responsibility due to the well-known "glass ceiling".

Among other disturbing observations is the increase in part-time work, which is especially prevalent among women with young children; other types of atypical work include temporary and occasional jobs, homework and subcontracting. Part-time workers are often young women who are less educated and less qualified than the average, which makes them more vulnerable. In Africa, in Asia and in Latin America, women are being called upon more and more to find work in the informal sector.

Even though some progress has been made in the area of wages, women's salaries are still between one-half and 80 per cent of those earned by men. Women's work is underestimated in most of the societies, and their income does not match their contribution to the economy. The difference in wages cannot be attributed to conditions of work alone. In the United States, in 1994, a woman in her twenties was likely to be earning 90 per cent of the rate of salary of her male counterpart.

Financial Problems

Financial problems and mentality issues emerged as two essential factors at every stage of the analysis of the causes of these persistent differences. The Forum's participants' general consensus was that they should be tackled first of all.

Financial implications cannot be separated from the issue of women's employment, whether it is to justify its need or on the contrary to discourage it, or to explain the absence or lack of training of women who are available in the job market. Some examples are:

- In the countries in transition in central and eastern Europe companies underpressure to increase profits, do not want to maintain social support services, which earlier had backed women's participation in the active population. These pressures are compelling women to leave the job market as the cost of childcare increases;
- In developing countries, especially in Asia, Africa and Latin America, the worsening of poverty and the increase in the number of single-parent families are requiring, women to turn towards income-generating activities, but the lack of training and dufficult access to credit constitute a major handicap;
- In Thailand, one of the major causes of young village girls resorting to prostitution is the state of poverty of their families, who are unable to afford secondary schooling for them.

Prejudices and Stereotypes

Several examples can also be found in the persisting traditions and stereotypes, which are an obstacle in the path of women's march to equality of opportunity in the world of work.

- The Nordic countries, in particular Sweden, have instituted a parental leave which enables either one of the parents to take care of the young children at home; but it can be noted that very few fathers avail themselves of this opportunity.

- The status of a profession falls as the number of women entering it increases; salary levels thus become relatively less competitive. This trend is particularly clear in the teaching professions and in some medical professions.
- Measures of positive action are becoming more and more general. They cannot be successful unless they tackle discrimination on all fronts, together with the fixed ideas that are prevalent on the subject of the sexes. In fact, solutions to the financial problems that women's work causes are themselves going through an evolution in mentalities.

In a highly competitive job market, opportunities available to women are conditioned by the comparative cost of women's labour, as it is perceived by the employer. By virtue of the legislation in force in the majority of countries, the obligations linked to maternity protection and family responsibilities tend to increase the direct costs of women workers; generally, employers bridge this gap by lowering the wages of women or limiting recruitment to childless women. This form of discrimination can also go as far as requiring medical certificates to guarantee sterility.

A Global Programme

To avoid such tendencies, efforts should be channelled toward two fronts. First, evaluating the relationship between a real cost-benefit (including the criterion of effective productivity) with a view towards eliminating the false idea that women workers are more expensive.

Secondly, making sure that in legislation, in practice and especially in the mentality of men and women all around the reproductive function and care of persons are recognised as social functions whose costs should be footed by society as a whole.

Recognising the universal nature of the problem and the various fronts where one would need to enter into combat, this programme should aim at changing the relationship of power between men and women. For this change to become permanent, it will be necessary to consolidate the ground gained as the process continues.

Remedies should be composed of measures touching upon, among other areas, legislation and its control, access to jobs, to training and to resources, the reconciling of professional activities with family responsibility, outreach measures to groups of underprivileged women, improvement of information and research, the participation of women in decision-making and the mobilisation of public opinion.

4

Women and Poverty

It is becoming more evident that the majority of the poor in developed and developing worlds are women. Poverty among rural women is growing faster than among rural men. Over the past 20 years, for example, the number of women in absolute poverty rose by 50 per cent as against some 30 per cent for rural men. The alarming evidence concerning the underlying trends for this process strongly indicates that the gender composition of the poor is veering towards a greater share of women.

Poverty manifests itself in many ways among migrant and refugee women, elderly women and children and indigenous women. Poverty is a complex, diverse and dynamic condition stemming out of depravation with respect to income, from social inferiority, isolation, physical weakness, powerlessness and humiliation.

Analysis of women's poverty suggest that its main causes stem from the perpetual disadvantage of women in terms of their position in the labour market, access to productive resources and income for the satisfaction of their basic needs. They also demonstrate that poor women possess exceptional resourcefulness, initiative and entrepreneurial spirit and that they show tenacity and self-sacrifice in trying to take a long-term view of their poor economic conditions and in safeguarding their livelihoods.

Development is the most important challenge facing the human race. The lack of progress in the last twenty years in the eradication of poverty and growing proportion of women among the poor is the single most important threat to the progress of development and its sustainability. As long as three-quarters of the world population continue to suffer from acute depravation, as long as profound imbalances in global consumption continue to persist, and, more important, as long as the spread of poverty, particularly among women, continues unchecked, there can be no development. The history of the development process shows again that the economic status of women is the key variable in the solution to the poverty crisis. It is time for the full recognition of the fact that women are part of the solution to poverty and to the stagnating development, not part of the problem.

The Earth Summit in Rio, the Human Rights Conference in Vienna, the Population Conference in Cairo and the Beijing Conference all were milestone events in terms of advancing our understanding of the crucial role of women in development and focusing the attention of the international community on the issues concerning the role of women in the work place and in society. All of them drew attention to women's full and effective participation in development. None, however, full articulated how to achieve this challenging task.

It is important to retain focus on the issue of economic potential when discussing poverty among women because it is clear that power is only meaning something in practical terms if it is reinforced by economic power. Women have the means to transform productive resources into such power if only enabling environment is created. It is not the lack of capabilities, but that of resources, which is clearly responsible for women's poverty.

Sometimes the so badly needed resources are not even truly scarce. Billions have been wasted on arms purchases around the globe and particularly in the countries, which can not afford such misallocation of public funds. At the same time, women's organisations from grassroots to the international level are poorly funded. Such misallocation of resources at the time when poverty among women is increasing, is immoral and unacceptable, not only on the part of the governments which pursue such wasteful policies, but also on the part of the suppliers, who in most cases are developed economies.

Government's responsibilities do not end here. It is extremely important, and indeed it is the main duty of every government around the world, to provide a conducive environment for economic growth and stability by pursuing responsible and sound macro-economic policies, which will enable the economy to grow without marginalizing women. When inflation is rampant, when political climate is unstable, leading to conflicts and civil strife, little can be done for poverty alleviation.

5

Promotion of Women

Women made up more than half the world's population, produced 80 per cent of its food, laboured for two-thirds of its working hours, were paid 10 per cent of its income and owned one per cent of its property.

These figures conceal manifold forms of the disadvantaging and discrimination of women. Such as the unjust division of burdens in families, the economic exploitation of women, the loss of their control over resources, and finally the unequal rating of paid and unpaid work. The latter, in the form of work for the family, on the land, for the community towards improving local living conditions, and nursing the old and the sick, adds up mostly to a 14 to 16 hour working day. True, employment of women has increased further everywhere in the world. But a number of them work in unsafe and socially unsecured conditions. They are also poorly paid and as a rule have hardly any chance to better themselves. Many women can earn money only in urban informal sectors or farming.

Global Public for Women

To be sure, the Decade of the Woman (1976 to 1985), the adoption of the convention on eliminating every form of discrimination against women (1979), the key role of women in the development process and their rights have created a global public for them. Moreover, their activities have got underway a reorientation of international policies on women. But, despite numerous progressive international moves in the area of formal legislation, the political debates on the legal status of women are in no way over.

Making general statements on the correlation of the impacts of social development and the situation of women is difficult because the political, economic and cultural frame-work conditions differ greatly from one country to another. However, discrimination against women manifests itself in most traditional as well as modern societies as a structural feature. Nowhere in the world are woman treated "as good" as men, and all countries slip on the scale of human development when inequality between the sexes is measured. Differences between the life situations and opportunities of men and women still arise from unequal possibilities of access to employment, income, economic resources, healthcare, food, education and training.

Social developments such as fundamental changes in traditional family and social structures, migration, urbanisation, the contrast between traditional and "modern" ways of life, and often unfavourable economic developments for the majority of the people have a great influence on the role of the woman in the various third world countries. Moreover, the increasing differentiation of the South in terms of poorer and richer countries cannot obscure the fact that in the 1990s the general social conditions for the majority of women have not improved.

Almost one-third of all the people in the countries of the South live in life-threatening poverty, and the overwhelming majority of those are women. Female poverty has different aspects, such as poverty of income, low literacy, a lack of vocational training and the poverty of old age.

Furthermore, the continuing legal pluralism in many societies impedes efforts to achieve equality of status for women. Although in many countries men and women are meanwhile equal according to the constitution and legislation, there is still a great contradiction between constitutionally guaranteed rights and reality. According to religious law or custom, women in many countries are not equal to men. That means they have no property rights, or may not sign any contracts without their husbands' and constitutional rights, this implies the danger of becoming poor, particularly for single mothers, divorcees or widows.

Against this background it is no surprise that women are under-represented at political decision-taking levels, in government posts, political parties, trade unions and associations. The structures of many institutions give little support to women's interests, and managerial positions are held almost exclusively by men. In part, women-specific measures are seen as a compulsory exercise and, at best, tolerated as a fad.

New Opportunities

But in general the radical changes taking place in many countries open new opportunities for policies on women. On the one hand, this is because the extent of the disadvantaging and suppression of women is more visible. And on the other, because the fields of work for women have become wider—if mainly in urban centres. In some countries, women have been able to push through binding legal regulations (election laws, political party statutes, women's quota rules for local councils), in order to guarantee their stronger participation in parties and trade unions. With the programme slogans of "empowerment" and "redistribution of power", women who are organised in self-help organisations, associations, networks and political parties are demanding participation in political decision processes and access to the political institutions. They are striving for social power in a bid to influence the factors which cause discrimination against them.

The transition from authoritarian to democratic forms of government in a great number of countries have placed women's organisations in a changed environment. There are now countless such bodies and their combined clout is changing the status of women and helping to broaden their scope for social action. But in some countries women are still faced with considerable difficulties in organising themselves with formal status.

On account of progressive impoverishment, however, the women's newly-wonscope for action and shaping their lives is markedly cramped. Current developments such as religious fundamentalism or economic recession have inhibiting impacts on new approaches to policies on women. In part, one must speak of a "backlash". Even where the legal position of women have been improved they have not been able to assert their social, economic and political rights. In some countries, it's feared that only elitist women's organisations will have a chance to break into the political process.

6

Women in Politics

Breaking Through the Barriers

The participation of women in political life is today on the agendas of most political parties in India. However, attempts to translate this goal into concrete reality have had limited success. A basic reason for this is the lack of conceptual clarity about the genuine commitment to the issue. For any such endeavour to be successful, it must be recognised that the equal participation of women and men in decision-making in all spheres is a prerequisite for effective democracy.

Participation means more than female membership in political parties, female voter turnout in elections or a token female presence in political bodies. Participation must be meaningful and effective, and must include representation in the political arena. This includes not only formal or higher level decision-making forums, but also other political units: the family, community groups, associations, trade unions and local bodies. These are crucial areas for intervention within which women can easily understand the issues and play an effective role.

The identification of barriers to women's political participation is obviously a prerequisite for overcoming them, but the visible barriers do not necessarily reflect the entire situation, and are often merely indicative of more deep-rooted problems. Governments tend to address the issue by devising measures capable of showing quick results. But tackling visible barriers without addressing their root causes results at best in temporary success.

Overcoming the barriers means not only eliminating them but also ensuring women's participation through other means. Affirmative action measures should not be perceived as privileges or concessions, but as interim measures to reverse existing imbalances, until such time as genuine equality and parity is achieved.

India must review its policies, constitution and legislation to see whether these have been discriminatory towards women, or have been ineffective in promoting women's rights. Since the issue of women's participation cannot be addressed in isolation, one must identify and assess factors affecting the development of a democratic culture or the recognition of human rights concerns. These factors include the country's political history, its socio-cultural, ethnic and religious diversity, the impact of traditional, customary, feudal and tribal laws, and the use of religious interpretations regarding women's rights.

One must review the prevalent general situation of women. While inequalities and imbalances exist in all places, some have stronger patriarchal structures wherein gender roles are more rigidly assigned. It is particularly important to assess women's political participation, including political rights, participation in election process and political parties; representation in legislative bodies and local councils, women in the civil service and in trade unions, and women's groups and lobbies.

Barriers to women's political participation can be legal, social, financial or political. In addition to identifying such barriers, it is useful to assess initiatives taken by governments and non-governmental organisations (NGOs), to evaluate successes and failures, identify the reasons and make modifications.

Based on the above, appropriate multi-pronged strategies and actions must be devised. It is important to develop a clear policy articulating the effective involving of women in the formulation of laws and policies which govern their lives.

Measures must be taken to ensure the principle of equality as a fundamental right. National legislation must be amended or repealed to remove any discriminatory provision. Positive legislation must be introduced to promote or protect affirmative action measures. The language of the law must clearly address itself to men and women, changing the practice of using the legal 'he' to include 'she'.

Research must be undertaken to cover information gaps. Monitoring mechanisms, guidelines and indicators must be devised and a process of periodic data collection established to assess changing trends. Documentation and analysis of innovative initiatives must be ongoing, to help in devising and modifying strategies.

Women's human rights and power sharing issues must be integrated in all training programmes of government, semi-government and autonomous institutions. Key personnel involved in decision-making and implementation need to be made sensitive to gender issues. Political education and training programmes for women are needed at the community level, for NGOs and community-based organisations, communicators, development workers and media personnel, etc.

Campaigns to change attitudes and social norms and project a positive image of women can be run through educational efforts and the media, and public discussions and debates. A clear stand should be taken against any misrepresentation of religion which stands in the way of women's equality and political participation.

Workshops and seminars should promote closer interaction between women in NGOs, advocacy and research groups, government departments, political leadership, trade unions, worker's associations and the media.

A minimum quota should be established for women in all sectors and grades of the civil service, including government, semi-government and autonomous organisations. A minimum percentage of key advisory positions, directorships, etc. should be reserved for women. Advertisements for government jobs should specifically state women's eligibility.

Electoral rolls should be systematically updated to include all eligible women. Education should be provided on electoral rights, political parties, election issues and concrete ways of holding candidates and political parties accountable. Political parties should publish their positions on women's rights issues, and encourage women to vote on issues that concern them. Constitutions of political parties should exclude provisions which condone or justify discrimination.

An adequate minimum representation of women in legislative bodies and local councils can be ensured by reserving seats through such means as putting women's names in priority positions on lists, providing financial support to female candidates, and making legal provisions that only those parties which give certain minimum number of tickets to women are eligible to contest elections.

A government ministry with the requisite authority should be designated as a focal point for devising policy, ensuring implementation and coordinating with other ministries and agencies.

An autonomous Permanent Commission on the Status of Women should be set up to function as a think tank on women's issues, to commission policy research and to review, recommend and monitor the implementation of policies and programmes in the field of development, rights and political participation. The commission should comprise government representatives, NGOs, human rights organisations and experts in different areas.

A judicial authority should expedite women's human rights cases; this could take the form of a human rights bench, a tribunal or an equality ombudsman. These are only some of the basic principles and guidelines that can be adopted. Ultimately, however, no strategy can be effective unless it is also backed by the requisite political will and impetus.

7

Women in Authority

The Ideal and the Reality

At the current rate of progress it will take a very long time to bring about equality in sharing decision-making between men and women in all areas. In terms of human rights and social justice, such equality is absolutely vital; it is also the best way to promote change with a human face. Would the world be a better place if women had equal access to management positions?

A Near Absence

Almost everywhere in the world, women have the vote and account for over half of the electorate. With but rare exceptions, however, their political activities are restricted to anonymous and informal roles in local communities. They hover at the margins of the higher levels of trade union, political, governmental and corporate life, and of interest groups. Until 1987, women occupied hardly 10 per cent of parliamentary seats. The same holds true for the trade unions, despite the fact that women account for nearly one-third of union memberships. Indeed, the women to have reached the leadership of a trade union can be counted on the fingers of one hand. This pattern of inequality is mirrored, indeed accentuated, in the employers' organisations, where women are practically absent. Everyone knows the situation in professional employment. Women continue to be concentrated in lower-qualified, lower-paid jobs, and very few manage to attain managerial posts, though the trend is on the increase.

Lower-paid Jobs

The "invisibility" of women in public life, and consequently in political, economic and professional activity, is both the cause and consequence of their being consistently barred from positions of authority. The way in which cultural and social models repeat themselves creates a setting that is hardly conducive to women progressing much beyond the limits of their homes and immediate working and living environment. Enmeshed in a tangle of little encouragement and probable reprobation, women are hesitant about struggling to advance in professional or political careers, as to do so would frequently put at stake the subordinate role that hitherto at least guaranteed them a secure position within the family circle. On the other hand, as they hardly manage to participate fully in the decisions affecting their lives and families, it will prove difficult for them to break out of the vicious circle.

Rights and Obstacles

Why is it then essential for women to play an equal role in decision-making? One can approach this objective from three points of view. First, it is a clear question of human rights: women make up half the population and more than one-third of the workforce and so their right to full citizenship and equality of opportunity and treatment in employment must be clearly expressed by their participating in all levels of activity. Secondly, it is a matter of social justice to combat discrimination against women, which is at its very harshest when it comes to employment. Thirdly, it is an essential requirement for the acceleration and effectiveness of development, as women are capable of providing a different sort of ability and creativity, which has not so far been tapped, and they can ensure a better balance in the allocation of resources and distribution of the benefits of progress.

Two Types of Obstacles

There are two types of obstacles to be overcome in order that women can have access to decision-making positions—structural and situational. These include the famous differences in levels of education, occupational experience and income levels as compared to men. These combine with and are reinforced by the situational factors such as the burden of family responsibilities, legal, psychological and material dependence on their spouses and male relatives, colleagues or bosses, and the fact that society is not prepared to change its attitudes and support women in assuming positions of responsibility. The deeply rooted "gender ideology" underlying all this constitutes a system of barriers to the upper echelons. It takes the form of values, attitudes and behavioural patterns which inhibit development and the recognition of the leadership qualities of women and which thus demand additional sacrifices from those who nevertheless strive to overcome them.

Additional Sacrifices

It has been estimated that women's participation in excess of 30 per cent in the upper echelons would be necessary for any noticeable difference to be made to the nature and tenor of the decisions taken in the areas affected. So what would this difference be? Women tend to speak with a "different voice" which as a rule lays stress on the social ethos of development, that is to say education, health, children, environment, dialogue and peace. Conversely, men tend to concentrate on the economic aspects such as production, trade, profitability, finance, technology and national defence. If we really aspire to any development of the human lot involving both economic growth and social equity, the best way to achieve this coveted objective will be by having men and women sharing in decision-taking.

❑ ❑ ❑

8

Empowerment for Women

The Gap Between Theory and Practice

Actually, the situation of women has changed completely in the last 30 years. At the beginning of the 1970s women were a blind spot in both development aid and the debate on it. The promotion of women is now established in all state institutions and non-governmental organisations (NGOs). Gender training is to sensitise development workers to take a gender-specific approach in analysing development processes, carrying out statistical surveys, and planning and evaluating activities.

From Integration to Empowerment

Those women who in the 1970s criticised development policy and its actors for being one-eyed must now see themselves as line-prompters and idea-providers. All the terms they used have been adopted in official usage. The image of the woman has changed from being a Cinderella-like, hard-done-by person, the poor soul, the victim, to a dynamic, reliable actor with apparently inexhaustible reserves of energy and creativity to bring to bear in a development process that has got stuck. The concept of empowerment has replaced the old "integration in development" approach in the promotion of women. And the women's approach (Gender and Development). This calls for the inclusion of men, taking a close look at the gender relationship and changing it into the long run.

All this undoubtedly progress which illuminates the blind spot. So is that enough to please women critics of the male-dominated development aid scene and female lobbyists for the promotion of women? Have they achieved what they wanted? That is a policy on women which on the one hand takes up their practical everyday needs, but on the other works strategically towards eliminating the hierarchy between the genders by structural changes? The fact is that one must differentiate between what governments, multilateral institutions and NGOs are saying and what they are doing.

Redistribution of Social Power and Control of Resources

The empowerment concept makes clear the political and economic gap between men and women. It aims at a redistribution of social power and control of resources in favour of women based on a development strategy which is no longer oriented on growth, the world market and military power.

The concept has had seemingly record acceptance in the executive suites and programmes of the governments while at the same time its substance has been drastically diluted. Taken on board hook-line-and-sinker by official policy, its politically critical teeth—namely posing the power question—have been extracted. It now has no bite critical of development and social policy. It just stands modestly and harmlessly for every strengthening and participation of women.

Professionalisation on the NGOs side and state-orientation on the grassroots have brought activities nearer to one another. The modes of expression are identical. But where are women really at the centre of development practice? And where are they at the centre of developmental ogranisations? The promotion of women is still an appendage to development policy, including in most NGOs. That is shown not only by the low number of "pure" women's projects, but also by the subordinate role of women's interests and measures for women in integrated programmes. Defined as a "cross-sectoral task" the advancement of women is often reduced to the mere addition of a women competent. For example, in the form of small-scale loans for sewing machines. The few women in the organisations are assigned a low-ranking and sparsely-equipped niche.

Lack of Long-term Strategy

The gender approach has made the yawning gap between rhetoric and practice even bigger. It might be useful as an instrument of analysis, if it is not debased to a technocratic checklist. But no one at present knows for sure how it can be implemented. The international trend is to implement promotion of women less in "pure" women's projects than to integrate it in other activities. Parallel to that, there are signs of a trend in which the women's or gender sections of development agencies are being disbanded and integrated in country or specialist sections. Currently, however, there is apparently still a lack of concepts for implementing a strategically oriented advancement of women. If integration, or "mainstreaming", now takes place at the various levels, it is to be feared that the promotion of women will peter out rather than spread.

At the same time, disenchantment prevails among those who have understood that the advancement of women is a means to more rights and opportunities in life, more self-confidence and social recognition. The demand to effect structural change through projects founders on the general conditions. Like development assistance as a whole, raising the status of women is also in many regions becoming increasingly merely disaster relief and survival aid. All involved have long known there are no universally applicable formulas for projects, and still fewer handy "directions for use" for getting out of poverty and blasting open patriarchal suppression.

The dilemma is clear. The economic crisis, the over-indebted and socially inactive governments, and the men who steal away from responsibility are saddling women with ever increasing burdens in securing survival. Thereby the women urgently need support. At the same time, the limited impacts of promotional measures, or even their boomerang effect, are becoming more obvious.

Many women are being catapulted into the exploitation mechanisms of the market and money economy only when they get involved in projects. Or, at least, the projects are speeding that process. Because of the projects the women neglect subsistence production and their traditional principles of the moral economy. But it is also clear that as a result of training programmes, new forms of organisation, development of new fields of action, and mobility, women's groups would collapse.

Thus, the old dilemma—of here a policy of small steps necessary for survival, and there big strategic and structural concepts—has got worse. But there's no way around it: the advancement of women must continue to seek bridges between being content with little and the vision of a development that is more just to women.

❑ ❑ ❑

9

For a Fair Sharing of Time

Women may have entered public life on a massive scale, but they are still on their own when it comes to running the household. A new balance must be struck if there is to be genuine democracy. At the dawn of the 21st century, states and the international community can no longer refute the fact that humanity is made up of two sexes, not just one. This discovery, a precious legacy of the century that just closed, has brought women's existence into the limelight. One of the great democratic challenges for societies over the next century will be to mature so that both sexes are able to live their lives on an equal footing, with all their differences, contrasting history and culture, but also with equal rights and responsibilities.

Women's rise to power and their participation in politics are the vital signs of a healthy democracy. If only this vision that emerged from the 1995 Beijing Women's Conference could spread wordwide, one can call it a radicalisation of democracy. When women take part in the public arena, contributing to the ongoing, shared effort to shape better ways of living together, a qualitative leap occurs. Their participation fills a gap which has until now prevented the emergence of a truly democratic culture.

Archaic Attitudes

But attitudes are not the only obstacle to women's ambitions. The structure of society and the way men and women run their daily lives are other stumbling blocks. The Inter-American Development Bank has had the good idea of giving the Institute for Cultural Action, and NGO in Rio de Janeiro, the task of setting up a pilot programme to train women for positions of political and social power. Participants include trade union and NGO leaders, key figures from the black and indigenous communities, company executives, civil servants and policymakers.

These women of different ages, educational backgrounds and ethnic origins are all aware of one fact: they are paying a very high price for a social contract that was negotiated when women were in a position of weakness, and agree that this has to change.

Re-mapping the Division Between Public and Private Life

In Rio de Janeiro revealed that there is an urgent need to reorganize the use of time, to strike a new balance between responsibilities and to re-map the division between public and private life. Household task must be recognised as time consuming, socially and economically vital and a serious check on women's ambitions.

Women in positions of power must constantly prove that they can behave like men. They keep quiet about having to look after children, run a household and care for elderly parents. Bringing those issues out into the open would mean admitting "flaws" that men do not have, for the simple reason that they delegate such work to their wives.

By drawing a veil of silence over their home life as if it were something illicit, women are allowing a basic fact to be hidden: the world of work relies on a domestic zone run by them. Women have changed, but the world of work has not and they are reaching the point of exhaustion. Filled with a deep sense of injustice, they are asking themselves. "Where did I go wrong?"

Understanding that humanity is composed of two different but equal sexes has several implications. Society must redefine itself because women are turning up in public carrying children in their arms and breast-feeding them, and because they have their own awareness and language that come from life experiences which are different from those of men.

An Untenable Double Burden

Articulating issues affecting public and private life is complicated, but that does not mean the equation is impossible of that the problems they raise should be brushed aside especially since the two worlds of public and private life are intertwined and mutually supportive. The balance between the two has now been upset. Women have entered public life on a massive scale, but the organisation of home life, how time is used and who is responsible for what tasks is still the same, as if nothing had changed. And yet such a world, where women are expected to soldier on just as before, "simply" adding to their lives experiences hitherto reserved to men, is called egalitarian.

That misunderstanding is fueled by an age-old tradition of dismissing the world of women, even by women themselves. Because society does not consider what they do in the home as having any major social significance, it fails to add this part of their lives to the other side of the equation.

This is why the massive migration of women from the home to the public arena is occurring without societies having to think seriously about how and by whom domestic work will be done in the future (and which women still do, but at what cost!). The double burden, resulting from an outdated social contract, is putting women under mounting pressure by speeding up their lives to an untenable pace. We are facing a social problem that society as a whole must solve and not, as many think, a problem that women must settle by working even harder.

As new areas of power open up to women, both sexes must take a fresh look at how they use time. Rearranging it is a challenge to society's imagination. But has this necessity sunk into the minds of decision-makers? I do not think so. This poses a major problem because it is a missing building block in the construction of our democracies.

The everyday work is proof of this. Women must put these issues on the political and economic agenda, thereby contributing to a more radical definition of democracy. Feminism's new demand for a different sharing of time also opens a debate that goes beyond the interests of women alone. In the final analysis, time and its constants define the limits of our own lives and the range of choices we make, in accordance with the meaning we give to our own existence.

The equality equation is increasingly complex. It is not enough to wipe out the last traces of discrimination in public life. A new definition of equality will emerge when both sexes start sharing responsibility in the private realm. Otherwise, the issue will be distorted and women will lose all chance of succeeding in public life.

10

What is Known About Reducing Maternal Mortality?

Historical records demonstrate the significant improvements that can be achieved when key interventions are in place. Reductions in maternal mortality took place in Sweden during the 1800s, for example, as a result of a national policy favouring professional midwifery care for all births, coupled with establishment of standards for quality of care. By the beginning of the 20th century, maternal mortality in Sweden was the lowest around 230 per 1,00,000 live births compared with over 500 per 1,00,000 in the mid-1880s. In Denmark, Japan, Netherlands, and Norway, similar strategies produced comparable results. In England and Wales, significant reductions in maternal mortality were not apparent until the 1930s; at the national level, political commitment to the strategy was achieved only slowly and the introduction of professional midwifery was correspondingly delayed. In every case, however, the key to these improvements was the institution of fully professional maternity care.

In the USA, where strategy focused on hospital delivery by doctors, maternal mortality remained high because it proved difficult to establish adequate regulatory frameworks and mechanisms to ensure quality of care. In 1930, the maternal mortality ratio in the USA was still 700 per 1,00,000 live births compared with 430 in England and Wales.

More recently, India witnessed significant reductions in maternal mortality in a relatively short period. From a level of over 1500 per 1,00,000 live births in 1940-1945, maternal mortality fell to 555 per 1,00,000 in 1950-1955, 239 per 1,00,000 within 10 years, and 95 per 1,00,000 by 1980. The figure is now 30 per 1,00,000. These improvements followed the introduction of a system of health facilities around the country allied to an expansion of midwifery skills and the spread of family planning. During the 1950s most births in India took place at home with the assistance of untrained birth attendants. By the end of the 1980s over 85% of all birth were attended by trained personnel.

Similar evidence of the effectiveness of health care interventions is available from China, Cuba, and Malaysia. These countries established community-based maternal health care systems comprising prenatal, delivery, and postpartum care and a system of referral to a higher level of care in the event of obstetric complications.

What these examples clearly demonstrate is that a country's overall economic wealth is not in itself the most important determinant of maternal mortality. There are numerous other examples of countries with modest levels of GNP which have achieved low maternal mortality.

❑ ❑ ❑

11

One Battle After Another

Women fought for their rights throughout the twentieth century. In the past several decades, their struggles has truly become global, but all is far from won. We often hear that this will be century of women, in light of the tremendous strides that have been made in the past thirty years or so. Although it is far too soon to confirm this prediction, it can safely be asserted that the twentieth century was marked by their struggle to leave the home, where they were confined by the ancestral division of roles along gender lines. Around the world, women have campaigned to win the rights they have been denied and to build, side-by-side with men, the future of the planet.

True, such struggles had already been waged in the past, although they were deliberately shunned in official historical accounts. But the brief revolts of this special "minority", which accounts for over half of humanity, did not change the place of women in their societies. They may have ruled the roost, sometimes enjoying undeniable respect, but nevertheless they were still born to serve men and bring their husbands' descendants into the world.

Education: Their First Struggle

Yet, at the start of the twentieth century, the traditional distribution of roles, seemingly legitimised by every religion and frozen in a "natural" order, began to crumble under the two-pronged assault of modernisation and women's struggle for their collective emancipation. They waged many battles to gradually obtain, despite set-backs, a change in their status—which is still far from achieved.

The first struggle of the twentieth century was for education. In 1861, a young woman graduated in Finance with a baccalaureate, a high school leaving examination, for the first time. In 1900, the first female university was founded in Japan. The same year, girls won the right to secondary education in Egypt and the first girl's school in Tunisia. Young women who could made the most of these new educational opportunities, not only to become better household managers and good educators for their children, as the main discourse of the period suggests, but also to do something unprecedented: to enter the forbidden spheres of public life, to exercise citizenship and to participate in politics. Throughout the twentieth century, women waged a battle on two fronts: by fighting for their own rights and taking part in the major social political emancipation movements.

The earliest feminist movements, which first appeared in the West in the late nineteenth century, focused on workplace and civil rights issues. Industry needed women's labour, which was underpaid in comparison with that of their male counterparts. 'Equal pay for equal work!' demanded American and European women, who began setting up their own trade unions and organizing strikes. They made unquestionable strides, but after more than one century of struggle, most women around the world still earn less pay for equal work.

The Right to Vote

The second objective of the twentieth century's pioneers was participation in public life, which hinged first and foremost on having the right to vote. The struggle was long and sometimes violent, as shown by the British "suffragettes" who demonstrated in the streets or Chinese women who made their demands heard by invading their country's new parliament in 1912. Everywhere, the fierce resistance of the political world progressively yieded to determined women's movements.

Control Over their Own Bodies

For a while, women's rights movements took a back seat to the Second World War and liberation struggles in the European colonies. The fight against fascism and, after 1945, colonialism, mobilised all their energy. Women distinguished themselves in these struggles, but that did not suffice to establish their rights as a gender. However, the world continued to change. With independence, many women in the South won access to schooling, salaried employment and, in a few exceptional cases, the closed world of politics. In Western countries, the post-war period saw them enter the workforce on a massive scale. The gap between social reality and the discriminatory laws defended by exclusively male power structures grew wider.

In the West, the second generation of feminists emerged in the wake of the libertarian movements of 1968. Picking up where their elders left off, they broadened the scope of their demands, for late-twentieth century feminists no longer aspired to the right to be "just like men" Challenging the claim of the "white male" to represent university, their goal was to achieve equality while remaining distinct as women. The women's liberation movement that first emerged in the American middle-class claimed the right to control one's own body. Feminists fought for contraception and abortion rights in many countries where one or both were against the law, and for autonomy and equality within the couple. "The personal is political", proclaimed women inspired by Marxism and psychoanalysis. "Workers of the world, who washes your socks?" chanted demonstrators in the streets of Paris in the 1970s. In France, the Veil Law legalizing abortion unleashed emotional debate in 1974.

Many Third World women could not identify with the struggles being waged in the West and insisted on leading their own battles at their own pace. However, these Western feminist movements breathed new life into the cause. Recognizing the changes and proclaiming their intention to accelerate them, the United Nations declared 1975 "International Women's Year" and organized the first international women's conference in Mexico City.

Already proclaimed in the Universal Declaration of Human Rights in 1948, sexual equality was reasserted in 1929 by the Convention on the Abolition of All Forms of Discrimination Against Women, which became a precious emancipation tool in the North as well as the South. At UN conferences in Copenhagen in 1980, Nairobi in 1985 and Beijing in 1995, women from both hemispheres found common ground, demanding the right to "have a child if I want it, when I want it," rejecting Malthusian principles and claiming their place in political bodies that until then had decided the world's future without them, struggling against religious fundamentalism that jeopardized their modest gains.

Misogyny of the Political Class

Of course, the struggle of Kuwaiti women against those who have denied that the right to vote or Indian women against the forced abortion of female foetuses is not the same as American women's battle against their own fundamentalists or French women's campaign against the misogyny take different approaches depending on the continent and do not necessarily have the same priorities, but the struggle has nonetheless become global during the past several decades. In the last twenty-five years, women have gradually increased their presence in public life, although it can hardly be said that the doors are wide open for them. From Africa to Asia, women's organisations have multiplied and acquired experience.

But their victories remain incomplete and the future is uncertain. From the nightmare of Afghan women to the ways in which equality is resisted in the so-called most advanced countries, the obstacles show that there is still a long way to go. Will women see the end of the struggle in this century that has just begun, the one which supposedly belongs to them?

12

Gender-based Violence

Around the world at least one woman in every three has been beaten, coerced into sex, or otherwise abused in her lifetime. Most often the abuser is a member of her own family. Increasingly, gender-based violence is recognised as a major public health concern and a violation of human rights.

The effects of violence can be deviating to a woman's reproductive health as well as to other aspects of her physical and mental well-being. In addition to causing injury, violence increases women's long-term risk of a number of other health problems, including chronic pain, physical disability, drug and alcohol abuse and depression. Women with a history of physical or sexual abuse are also at increased risk for unintended pregnancy, sexually transmitted infections and adverse pregnancy outcomes. Yet victims of violence who seek care from health professionals often have needs that providers do not recognise, do not ask about, and do not know how to address.

What is Gender-based Violence?

Violence against women and girls includes physical, sexual, psychological and economic abuse. It is often known as "gender-based" violence because it evolved in part from women's subordinate status in society. Many cultures have beliefs, norms and social institutions that legitimise and therefore perpetuate violence against women. The same acts that would be punished if directed at an employer, a neighbour, or an acquaintance often go unchallenged when men direct them at women, especially within the family.

Two of the most common forms of violence against women are abuse by intimate male partners and coerced sex, whether it takes place in childhood, adolescence, or adulthood. Intimate partner abuse—also known as domestic violence, wife-beating and battering—is almost always accompanied by psychological abuse and in one-quarter to one-half of cases by forced sex as well. The majority of women who are abused by their partners are abused many times. In fact, atmosphere of terror often permeates abusive relationships.

How Health Care Providers Can Help?

Health care providers can do much to help their clients who are victims of gender-based violence. Yet providers often miss opportunities to help by being unaware, indifferent, or judgemental. With training and support from health care systems, providers can do more to respond to the physical, emotional and security needs of abused women and girls.

First, health care providers can learn how to ask women about violence in ways that their clients find helpful. They can give women empathy and support. They can provide medical treatment, offer counselling, document injuries and refer their clients to legal assistance and support services.

Family planning and other reproductive health care providers have a particular responsibility to help because:

- Abuse has a major—although little recognised—impact on women's reproductive health and sexual well-being;
- Providers cannot do their jobs well unless they understand how violence and powerlessness affect women's reproductive health and decision-making ability;

- Reproductive health care providers are strategically placed to help identify victims of violence and connect them with other community support services.

Providers can reassure women that violence is unacceptable and that no woman deserves to be beaten, sexually abused, or made to suffer emotionally.

Societal Responses

Health workers alone cannot transform the cultural, social and legal environment that gives rise to and condones widespread violence against women. Ending physical and sexual violence requires long-term commitment and strategies involving all parts of society. Many governments have committed themselves to overcoming violence against women by passing and enforcing laws that ensure women's legal rights and punish abusers. In addition, community-based strategies can focus on empowering women, reaching out to men and changing the beliefs and attitudes that permit abusive behaviour. Only when women gain their place as equal members of society will violence against women no longer be an invisible norm but, instead, a shocking aberration.

❑❑❑

13

Sex and Gender

A World of Difference

Understanding the differences between women and men, and how they are determined, is of key importance in understanding why a gender perspective is so important for development and the elimination of world poverty.

Differences between women and men are determined by biology, on the one hand, and society, on the other.

- Sex marks the distinction between women and men as result of the fundamental biological, physical and genetic differences between them.
- Gender roles are set by convention and other social, economic, political and cultural forces.

The precise boundary between these factors is the subject of fierce debate. Some people believe that the only important difference is that women can bear children and men cannot. Others believe that biology determines a much wider set of characteristics, attributes and capabilities. Whatever the case, the wide variation in the position of women in different societies around the world demonstrates that, unlike sex, gender roles are by no means fixed by nature—they are made by people, and can be renegotiated and changed.

The position of women in society is far from being of academic interest alone. It not only has fundamental consequences for the quality of life of both women and men, but also has a direct impact on a society's prosperity and well-being. The government's policy on international development recognises that gender-based inequality is a major obstacle to the escape from poverty. Studies have shown that developing countries which strive to ensure that women have equal rights have higher rates of economic growth, lower mortality rates, smaller and healthier families, and a better-educated population. Changing gender roles can make a world of difference.

The evidence also shows that gender equality is not a luxury which can only be afforded by rich countries. UN data reveals that some developing countries outperform much richer ones in the opportunities they afford women. The better performing countries are scattered throughout the world, showing that culture and religion need not be barriers to the advancement of women.

The gender gap in many countries is closing fast. Rapid progress has been made in recent decades. But in no society do women fare as well as men. Women are gaining ground in health and education terms, but still have a long way to go in sharing political and economic opportunities. They continue to suffer high levels of violence and abuse, and in many countries are treated differently to men by the law. These disadvantages are not due to sex differences, but are the result of gender discrimination.

Empowerment, Equality and Equity: What Do They Mean?

Women's empowerment, gender equality and equity are key terms in debates about the changes required in the relationships between women and men.

- *Empowerment* means individuals acquiring the power to think and act freely, exercise choice, and to fulfil their potential as full and equal members of society.
- *Equality* means that women should have the same rights and entitlements as men to human, social,

economic and cultural development, and equal voice in civil and political life. It does not mean that everyone should be the same, or that the benefits of development should be shared in exactly equal proportions by everyone. This would be neither feasible nor desirable, and would not be consistent with the notion of empowerment, which upholds everyone's right to determine their own future and the lifestyle of their choice.

- *Equity* means that the exercise of these rights should lead to outcomes which are fair and just, and which enable women to have the same power as men to define and pursue the objectives of development and shape societies of the future.

The difference between equality and equity is important because it underlines the rights of women to define the objectives of development for themselves and to seek outcomes which are not necessarily identical to those sought or enjoyed by men. Women have the right to pursue development paths which reflect their own needs and aspirations.

Upholding these rights is in the interests of men as well as women, because of the wider social and economic benefits brought by gender equality. Because of the universal disadvantages experienced by women, their empowerment is crucial to the achievement of equality and equity, the elimination of poverty and a better world for all.

14

Safe Motherhood is a Human Rights Issue

The death of a woman during pregnancy or childbirth is not only a health issue but also a matter of social injustice. Of the human rights currently acknowledged in national constitutions and in regional and international human rights treaties, many can be applied to safe motherhood. Many such treaties and conventions are based on the 1948 Declaration of Human Rights; They include (1) the Convention on the Elimination of All Forms of Discrimination against Women, (2) the Convention on the Rights of the Child, (3) the European Convention for the Protection of Human Rights and Fundamental Freedoms, (4) the American Convention on Human Rights, and (5) the African Charter on Human and Peoples' Rights (6).

Human rights of relevance to safe motherhood can be grouped into the following four principal categories:

- *Rights relating to life, liberty and security of the person,* which require governments to ensure both access to appropriate healthcare during pregnancy and childbirth, and women's rights to decide whether, when, and how often to bear children. Governments must therefore address factors within the economic, legal, social and health systems that deny women these fundamental rights.
- *Rights relating to the foundation of families and of family life,* which require governments to provide access to health-services and other facilities that women

need to establish families and to enjoy life within a family.

- *Rights relating to healthcare and the benefits of scientific progress, including health information and education,* which require governments to provide access to good sexual and reproductive healthcare with appropriate referral systems. The measures needed to ensure safe motherhood can be provided through primary healthcare irrespective of a country's level of economic development. Central to these rights is information on a range of reproductive health issues, including family planning, abortion and sex education.
- *Rights relating to equality and non-discrimination,* which require governments to provide access to services such as education and healthcare without discriminatory grounds such as sex, marital status, age and socio-economic class. Discriminatory policies include requirements for a woman to obtain the consent of her husband for particular healthcare interventions, requirements for parental authorisation which have a differential impact on girls, and laws that criminalise medical procedures that only women need. Governments are in violation of their obligations when they fail to implement laws that effectively protect women's interests or to allocate health resources to meet women's particular need for safe pregnancy and childbirth.

The actions that governments need to take to promote safe motherhood as a human right fall into three groups:

- *Reform of laws* that prevent women from attaining the highest possible levels of health and nutrition needed for safe pregnancy and childbirth and that inhibit access to reproductive health information and services such as laws requiring women in need of health care to seek the authorisation of husbands or other family members first.

- *Implementation of laws* that foster women's right to good health and nutrition and that protect women's health interests such as laws that prohibit child marriage, female genital mutilation, rape and sexual abuse. Every effort should be made to implement laws that encourage the healthy timing of births, such as those that support the education of girls, set a minimum age for marriage and ensure women's access to essential health care.
- *Application of human rights* in national legislation and policy to advance safe motherhood.

❑ ❑ ❑

15

Action for Safe Motherhood

Countries vary enormously in terms of the situations and challenges they face and their capacity to address these. However, experience from around the world over the past decade has demonstrated that a number of features are common to successful efforts to address maternal mortality. Reducing maternal mortality requires coordinated, long-term efforts. Actions are needed within families and communities, in society as a whole, in health systems, and at the level of national legislation and policy. Further, interactions among the interventions in these areas are critical to reducing maternal mortality and to building and supporting momentum for change.

Legislative and Policy Actions

Changes in legislation and policy are essential to ensure safe motherhood. Long-term political commitment is an essential prerequisite. When decision-makers at the highest levels are resolved to address maternal mortality, the resources needed will be mobilized and the essential policy decisions will be taken. Without this level of commitment over the long term, projects cannot become programmes and activities cannot be sustained.

A supportive social, economic, and legislative environment allows women to overcome the various obstacles that limit their access to health care, such as distance from their homes to appropriate health facilities, lack of transport and, more critically, financial and social barriers. Proper maternal health care is limited when women have to pay for services and essential drugs, and when they must bear substantial hidden costs such as time lost for housework, paid employment, food production, and child care. Legislation that supports women's access to care must be formulated to permit health workers at the periphery of the health system to perform specific life-saving functions. Failing this, only highly skilled health professionals, based largely in urban centres, can provide such care, and only women with sufficient money and the means to reach such centres can benefit from it.

With these objectives, careful review of national laws and policies is necessary, particularly in the following areas:

- ***Family Planning:*** Statutes that restrict women's access to family planning services (e.g. by requiring that a woman be married or that she should have her husband's approval) should be repealed. Policies must ensure that all couples and individuals have access to good-quality, voluntary, client-oriented, and confidential family planning information and to services that offer a wide choice of effective contraceptive methods. Policies should address regulatory, social, economic, and cultural factors that limit women's control over sexuality and reproduction, in order that pregnancies that are too early, too late, or too frequent may be avoided.

- ***Adolescents and Children:*** Policies and programmes should encourage late marriage and child-bearing and an expansion of the economic and educational opportunities for girls and women. Promotion of good nutrition in childhood and adolescence, as well as supplementation if necessary during pregnancy, provides protection for both women and their future children. Policies should also enable adolescents to take responsibility for and protect their sexual and reproductive health, and facilitate their access to health information and services. All children, before they reach the age at which they become sexually active, need to be taught the risks of unprotected sex and helped to develop the skills needed to protect themselves from sexual coercion.

- ***Barriers to Access:*** Assigning health workers trained in midwifery to village-based health facilities can help overcome problems of distance and transport. Health workers should also be trained to deal sympathetically with women patients. Policies should support the provision of services at minimum cost, at the same time, health workers should have job security, be paid adequate wages, and be provided with sufficient supplies to do their jobs. Policies that will increase women's decision-making power, particularly in regard to their own health, are also essential.
- ***Regulation of Practice:*** Protocols and statutes aimed at providing both routine maternal care and referral facilities for obstetric complications at each level of the health system need to be developed. Responsibilities at each level for supervision, deployment of health care personnel, remuneration, and reporting procedures must be defined nationally. Development and promotion of education and training curricula are important, as is the setting of national norms and standards to govern the selection of trainees, trainers, and supervisors.
- ***Delegation of Authority:*** Services should be decentralized so that facilities are available as close to people's homes as possible. Adequate supplies and equipment and trained staff should be available in all health facilities, particularly in rural and remote areas, together with written policies and protocols to guide service provision and to allow certain functions to be delegated to personnel at lower levels (when appropriately trained).

- ***Abortion:*** Availability of services for management of abortion complications and post-abortion care should be ensured by appropriate legislation. Where abortion is not prohibited by law, facilities for the safe termination of pregnancy should be made available. National policy can discourage unsafe abortion practices by promoting protection against unwanted pregnancy, and national helath campaigns to publicize the risks of unsafe abortion and the need to recognize and seek treatment for abortion complications.

16

Population Growth and Women's Role in India

We have limited economic resources. There is a pressing need to abolish poverty. If population grows unchecked, abolition of poverty becomes very difficult. Due to the rise in population, illiteracy is growing as educational facilities are not expanding as fast as the population. Though employment facilities are being provided, we are not able to solve the unemployment problem. Though production and national income are rising, standard of living is not rising at the same rate. Thus growing population remains a serious drawback.

Conventional wisdom holds that slowing population growth is the key to solving a vast array of social, economic and environmental problems. To be sure, in a world of finite resources, unlimited growth in the number of people requiring food, shelter and work, not to mention access to natural resources, cannot be sustained. But the increasingly singular focus on demographics simply deflects attention from the fundamental social conditions—poverty, inequity, and the abject status of women, of which population growth is not the cause, but the consequence.

In India, as in much of the world, women are last in line for education, job training, credit, and sometimes even food—despite the fact that raising the status of women is the most effective way both to reduce birth and to achieve higher standards of health and economic productivity.

In India's tradition-bound society, where child-bearing is often the only route to status and security, the majority of women have little to gain from having fewer children. The government, by contrast, is bent on cutting birth rates to half over the next decade, but has shown little commitment to meeting women's needs. And so a vicious cycle is perpetuated. As long as the status of women remains low, voluntary family planning efforts will continue to founder, tempting the government to use pressure to meet its demographic goals.

India will surpass China as the world's most populous country by the middle of the next century. Each day the number of people who lack access to adequate food, healthcare, housing, clean water and education spirals upward.

Female Education

Female education is the single most influential determinant of both lower birthrates and increasing empowerment for women.

Indian society manages to devote fewer resources to educating its girls than its boys. At the household level, cultural restrictions on female behaviour combined with the need for cheap household labour create a sharp gender gap in literacy. In both Hindu and Moslem traditions, for example, notions of female "modesty" and "purity" dictate that unmarried females remain separate from unrelated males. Because the bulk of India's teachers are men, and most schools educate boys and girls under the same roof, many traditional families keep their daughters home, regardless of their income. Moreover, parents opt to invest in educating girls only when they perceive that long-term gains will outweigh immediate costs.

For the impoverished majority, the expense of sending a girl to school—paying for uniforms, books especially when young girls are required to work at home and in the fields.

Women's lack of knowledge translates directly into poor nutrition and health for themselves and their offspring. In turn, this condition causes high infant mortality for which many women compensate by having more babies.

Nutrition and Health

Nutritional and health status is also marked by gender disparity. Both boys and girls in India are nutritionally at disadvantaged, as nearly half of the country's households fail to provide even the minimum daily caloric requirements. But malnutrition is far more prevalent among females than males. From birth, male children consistently receive more and better food than their sisters, even though the nutritional needs of prepubescent boys and girls are virtually identical. Boys, given the same level of illness, are taken to doctors more often than girls. As a result of this neglect, far more girls than boys die in the critical period between infancy and at age five.

Discrimination in feeding and healthcare produces one of India's most provocative signs of gender bias. In fact, the ratio of women to men in the country has been declining.

Women and Family Income

Son preference and the subsequently biased allocation of family resources is based on a series of myths the Indian government has failed to combat. One is the notion—not peculiar to India—that females do not contribute to family income. Throughout the world, women bear the "invisible" burdens of upaid domestic work and childbearing, the economic value of which is rarely reflected by official statistics.

Young girls in India generally work longer hours than boys of the same age. By age 10, girls in low income families are working eight or more hours a day assisting their mothers by tending siblings, collecting water and firewood, herding small animals, weeding fields, or facing the daily grind of low-paid child labour in the marketplace.

The poorer the family, the more vital the economic contribution that women and girls make, especially in the growing number of female-headed households.

Indifference Towards Women

The attempts to enhance agricultural productivity disproportionately benefit men.

Expansion of the irrigated area allocated to cash crops, such as groundnut and cotton, has come at the expense of food crops on which women depend to feed their families. And while the mechanisation of ploughing and levelling that comes with these projects reduces the traditional workload of men, that for women actually increases. Women still must carry out by hand the tasks of weeding, turning soil, and harvesting, but over much larger areas.

The result is to deepen women's poverty and enhance the perceived value of having many children to help with chores.

Not surprisingly, the share of married couples of reproductive age using contraceptives—now 40 per cent—is low, and most of these are older couples who turned to sterilisation (counted as a form of contraceptive) only after having large families.

This bleak situation is shadowed by an ominous fact of history. Past attempt to reduce births in the absence of social changes enhancing women's status have been accompanied by increases in violence against females—in the beating and abandonment of women who don't bear sons, in female infanticide and child neglect, and in the rising use of abortion for sex selection.

Experience shows that even in India, with its immense tangle of troubles, well-designed programmes can produce dramatic improvements in family health while improving women's status and reducing births.

Increasing young girls' access to education and offering older women a chance for learning are essential to increasing female autonomy. Requisite steps include serious efforts to train and hire more female teachers, to set up literacy and tutoring campaigns in every state, and to encourage the growth of women's empowerment groups to foster changes at the village level. These strategies already have been proven in the southern state of Kerala, internationally lauded for its dramatic gains in the health and economic status of women and in slowing population growth.

Equally important are broad public education campaigns to raise awareness of the immense value of women's work and welfare to families and societies. The mass media also could be enlisted in the effort to change dramatically social perceptions of women's roles by depicting positive images of women and their economic contribution to society.

Much of the battle to win recognition of the importance of women's lives and health to societies will have to be fought by women themselves. Indications are that women are responding to the challenge.

By filling the existing demand for quality voluntary family planning services, the government can make cuts in birthrates of at least 25 per cent over the next decade, thereby starting the process towards reducing the country's population. Equally critical to a long term strategy of sustainable development is a sustained political commitment to improve the status of women throughout India. Only by working towards all these objectives simultaneously can the dreams of women for full partnership in society come true.

17

Technological Entrepreneurship

The New Force for Economic Growth

Entrepreneurship has emerged as a major new force for change. The dynamic role of modern small business in economic growth has received fresh recognition worldwide. It is essential to promote entrepreneurship and to mobilize the dynamism of the private sector for accelerated national development. An unbridled private sector may not, however, ensure growth with equity. It is the prime responsibility of governments to create policy frameworks that enable business to apply technology for competitive advantage and for the well-being of the public.

The Changing Global Environment

As agents of change and progress, entrepreneurs start by identifying a market opportunity and matching this with social or technical innovations. They then proceed to mobilize the resources necessary to drive their business concept to its commercial realisation. The development of a product or service with a high-technology content—never easy anywhere, or at today's rapidly-changing global environment. It calls for restructuring the available technology and business development systems and developing the skills needed by a new breed of "techno-entrepreneurs" to transform innovations into market opportunities at home and abroad. It also requires reorienting the present processes and priorities of technical and economic cooperation among countries.

Amidst the global concerns of environmental preservation, poverty elimination and social development, the practical problems of entrepreneurship are not being properly addressed, even though entrepreneurs will create the bulk of enterprises, jobs and wealth.

A torrent of technology-based goods hits the market every week, ostensibly improving the quality of our lives while simultaneously creating complexity and dislocation. The pace of progress in information technologies, microelectronics, robotics, new materials, biomedical sciences, space science and other advanced technologies quickens, significantly changing the way we live. The growth of markets for these technologies also proceeds apace.

Further, technological change is taking place today against a background of growing intra-national and international disequilibria. While the transformation from State-centred to market-oriented development is opening up enormous opportunities and options, it has also caused severe short-term hardships. In order to survive and prosper in these changing times, India and its enterprises need enlightened government policies, good technical infrastructure and strong cultural roots.

Traditional production factors are giving way to a new paradigm characterised by new patterns of trade, investment and employment, and by informal networking life-long learning and technological entrepreneurship. The manufacturing sector in India continues to be dominated by food products, textiles, chemicals and other traditional industry, mainly in the public sector. However, change is coming, albeit slowly. State enterprises are being corporatised pending privatisation, and the share of knowledge-based and information-related activities in the marketplace is rising perceptibly. Restructuring policies now place emphasis (often purely rhetorical) on the role of the private sector. The legacy of decades of centrally-planned development is generally inimical to private enterprise. In turn, the private sector has been slow to respond to economic liberalisation in India and generally failed to generate the new employment necessary to absorb new entrants to the labour force.

The regulatory problems of an onerous tax structure and administration, poor access to finance and raw materials, over-regulation of labour and land use, pervasive bureaucracy and restricted markets have been significant barriers to entrepreneurial growth.

Towards Competitive Performance

The imperative of improved performance has serious implications for India if it is to survive, stay abreast and succeed. It calls for national efforts on systemic efficiency and productivity growth, the move from an investment-driven to an innovation-driven economy and sustained higher-order competitiveness; towards enhanced customer satisfaction at home and penetration of selected markets abroad. Concurrently, governments and business have to address such intractable problems as poverty, corruption and the degradation of the environment.

Creating New Technology-based Ventures

Starting a new business in India is a hazardous task. Problems are compounded when the venture is technology-based:

- Capital requirements are generally larger, while traditional banks are ill-equipped to process the perceived risk. Venture capital generally only becomes an option when the venture has documented the merits of its management, market and innovation;
- Knowledge-based ventures can benefit from linkages to sources of knowledge—e.g. the technical university or research lab. Such mentoring needs to be cultivated;
- Techno-entrepreneurs often have technical skills but usually lack the business management and marketing skills necessary for success. These need to be supplemented;

- In fields where technology is changing rapidly, it is often advantageous to make technology-acquisition arrangements. Sourcing such innovations, negotiating technology licensing agreements and protecting the intellectual property itself require special skills;
- Knowledge-based innovations are inherently more risky than others. The management of this unique risk requires assessment techniques and vision;
- Technology-based ventures often have social and environmental implications, which need to be managed carefully;
- Penetrating a competitive market requires good market intelligence, a good strategic plan and good luck.

Special Characteristics of "Techno-entrepreneurs"

The popular misconceptions are that techno-entrepreneurs are born, not made; that they take risks with other people's money and fail more often than they succeed. In fact, entrepreneur skills can be identified and developed. The entrepreneur is typically an innovator who formulates new solutions to existing problems, mobilizes resources and stimulates others to participate in his or her team. These aptitudes develop over time, often starting in childhood, as the person faces new challenges and learns from failure.

Entrepreneurial opportunities can be found in every industrializing country, community and family. Principal sources of entrepreneurs for knowledge-based ventures are often the university and government research laboratories, the large industrial and military establishments and professional service firms. Some motivations of the entrepreneur are the need to: be independent; create value; contribute to society; earn recognition; become rich or; quite often, simply not to be unemployed. Value-adding ventures with good growth potential can best be developed in an open market and in a culture which supports risk-taking.

The techno-entrepreneur anywhere has the challenge of moving a concept through the prototype and production phases towards creation of a product which meets market needs at a price consistent with the value created and with the ability of customers to pay.

Equally important, the market itself has to be developed and sustained. It is not enough to be first with a better mousetrap if one does not have the skills to educate and reach potential buyers and to set the market standard.

Hence one has to distinguish between innovators and inventors. The inventor is typically a creative person in a quest for knowledge or for producing new products, without determining in advance whether a real market exists for his or her inventions. On the other hand, the innovator draws on existing knowledge and the talents of others to develop or adapt a product or service at a volume and cost that can capture a significant portion of an identified market. The flexibility and creativity of a small entrepreneurial techno-venture may lead to more incremental and break-through innovations than can be generated by larger-sized firms in many sectors.

The pace and pattern of India's economic development now depend in large measure on its technical resource base. In this context, the key determinants are the skills to apply technology for enhanced competitiveness, as well as to create techbased ventures. Techno-entrepreneurs have to be supported by appropriate national structures and international linkages if they are to survive and flourish in an intensely competitive world.

18

The Biggest Industry the World Has Ever Seen

The Future of World Tourism

The year 2020 will see the penetration of technology into all aspects of life. It will become possible to live one's days without exposure to other people, according to WTO's latest look into the future.

But this bleak prognosis has a silver lining for the tourism sector. People in the high-tech future will crave the human touch and tourism will be the principal means to achieve this.

Tourism companies that manage to provide "high-touch" products will prosper. Upscale, luxury services that pamper and spoil their customers have a bright future in the upcoming century. But WTO's report also predicts good prospects for low-budget destinations and packages. Self-catering holiday facilities, for example, which offer plenty of opportunities for socialising among families and friends. Opportunities abound at both ends of the spectrum and there will be plenty of them.

$5 Billion a Day Industry

WTO's Study Tourism: 2020 Vision predicts 1.5 billion tourists will be visiting foreign countries annually by the year 2020, spending more than US $2 trillion or US $5 billion every day. These forecasts represent nearly three times more international tourists than the 66 million recorded in 1999 and nearly five times more tourism spending, which last year topped US $453 billion. Tourist arrivals are predicted to grow by an average 4.3 per cent a year over the next two decades, while receipts from international tourism will climb by 6.7 per cent a year.

To factor in domestic tourism, WTO multiplies arrivals by 10 and quadruples receipts, which brings us to the grant totals of 16 billion tourists spending US $8 trillion in 2020.

Tourism in the 21st century will not only be the world's biggest industry, it will be the largest by far that the world has ever seen. Along with its phenomenal growth and size, the tourism industry will also have to take on more responsibility for its extensive impacts. Not only its economic impact, but also its impact on the environment, on societies and on cultural sites, all of which will be increasingly scrutinised by governments, consumer groups and the travelling public.

We hope that Tourism 2020 Vision will be more than a useful marketing tool, that it will act as a warning signal for destinations—helping them recognise the need to prepare for the pressure of growth, WTO is advising destinations to implement long-term, strategic planning and to strengthen the partnerships, both strategically and at the operational level, between the public and private sectors.

Growth of Long-Haul

Tourism: 2020 Vision indicates that tourists of the 21st century will be travelling further afield on their holidays, often to China and even to outer space. The percentage of long-haul travel is predicted to increase from 18 per cent in 1995 to 24 per cent by 2020.

Tourism companies looking to cash in on this booming sector are advised to look towards Asia. China will be the world's number one destination by the year 2020 and it will also become the fourth most important generating market.

Currently it does not even figure among the world's destinations predicted to make great strides in the tourism industry are Russia, Hong Kong, Thailand, Singapore, Indonesia and South Africa.

Short pleasure voyages to outer space will become a reality by 2004 or 2005, according to the study carried out by WTO Statistics Chief Enzo Paci in consultation with 85 governments and 50 tourism visionaries.

It is expected space trips will last up to four days and cost on average US $100,000. NASA, the US space agency, has recently surveyed the travel industry for interest in space tourism and some US companies are already taking reservations and deposits from private citizens hoping to become the first tourists in outer space.

But while some travellers may be suiting up for space voyages, the vast majority of the world's population will never leave their own countries, not even by the year 2020.

Only 7 per cent of the world's population will be travelling internationally by the year 2020, up from 3.5 per cent in 1996—but still just the tip of the iceberg.

European Trends

Tourism: 2020 Vision predicts that Europe will remain by far the leading inbound tourism region as well as the main generator of international tourists. International arrivals in Europe will reach 717 million by 2020, more than twice as many as last year.

Overall, tourism to Europe is predicted to grow more slowly than the world average; at a rate of 3.1 per cent annually, though some countries will fare better than others. Central and Eastern European countries will become the new motor for Europe, feeding and being fed by other European and long-haul generating markets. Tourism to Central and Eastern Europe will grow by 4.8 per cent a year and the former Soviet Block countries will surpass 200 million arrivals by 2016—a doubling in last 15 years.

The Eastern Mediterranean countries of Cyprus, Turkey and Israel are also expected to show good growth of 4.6 per cent a year. Tourism to the United Kingdom is forecast to grow by 4 per cent annually, just under the world average. Reflecting world patterns and increasing air travel, Europeans will be taking trips more frequently and further from home. Total outbound travel from European countries is predicted to reach 771 million trips a year by 2010, again more than twice as many as last year.

Long-haul travel to countries outside of Europe will grow by 6.1 per cent a year in the upcoming decades to reach 15 per cent of all trips taken by Europeans or 115,600,000 departures. Long-haul currently accounts for 12 per cent of European outbound travel or about 42 million trips a year.

Since the typical European tourist who spends his holiday at the beach will be more frequently choosing Asian or Caribean resorts, European beach destinations are advised to orientate their product development and marketing increasingly to new tourist sources, especially Japan, the newly industrialised countries of Asia and the Americas.

Mature European destinations will have continually to strive to seek product and market differentiation to avoid a tired or stale image in major generating markets.

Recipe for Success

While growth of the tourism industry will be unstoppable in the 21st century, increased benefits cannot be taken for granted. Competition among destinations will also become increasingly fierce.

The Study Tourism: 2020 Vision outlines a series of 12 megatrends that will shape the sector and offers advice on how to better compete. No destination or tourism operator can afford to sit back and wait for more tourists to arrive. They have to be won—and there will be winners and losers. To be a winner, there are a number of imperatives:

1. Development focused on quality and sustainability;
2. Value for money;
3. Full utilisation of information technology to identify and communicate effectively with market segments and niches.

Product development and marketing will need to match each other more closely, based on the main travel motivators of the 21st century. *Tourism: 2020 Vision* calls these motivating factors the Three E's—Entertainment, Excitement and Education.

The study also highlights the importance of image in a tourists' selection of a holiday destination in the future. While an image of safety and security is already an important deciding factor for tourists, holiday makers of the 21st century will be looking for places with a trendy image.

As 2020 Vision points out, the next century will mark the emergence of the tourism destinations as 'a fashion accessory'. The choice of holiday destination will help define the identity of the travellers and, in an increasingly homogeneous world, set him apart from the hordes of other tourists.

Boutique destinations and space agencies beware! You are on the threshold of meeting the 21st century tourist.

19

Child Labour in Weaving Industry

Approximately 1,30,000 children work in India's hand-knitted carpet industry. The working conditions are often poor, involving long hours sitting in one position, breathing cotton and wool fibres, eye-strain from doing very fine work and poor lighting. In the smallest enterprises the only light often available is the natural light filtering in through an open doorway.

Children are more likely to work in larger establishments: the smallest enterprises are family operations where the father and other family members might both weave carpets and till a plot of land, whereas the larger buisness use almost all hired labour. In the one-loom enterprises, approximately 14 per cent of weavers are children, while the number of a child labourers rises to around 33 per cent in businesses with five or more looms.

Although the proportion of child labour rises with the size of firm, the proportion does not rise as the quality of carpet increases; in fact, children are more likely to work on low-quality than on the highest-quality carpets. There is "no evidence that children dominate any particular design or quality niches". The opposite would be the case if the "nimble fingers" argument were true.

If the "nimble fingers" argument does not hold in the hand-knitted carpet industry, then it probably does not hold in other industries. Rejection of the "nimble fingers" argument is reinforced by the ability of adults to master carpet-weaving skills. Many adolescents and young adults who attend government training centres go on to run their own weaving businesses, while weavers say it takes a year to become fully proficient, whether one starts as an adult or a child.

Enterprises Often Small and Impoverished

The workforce of the hand-knitted carpet industry is mired in poverty. Most weaving enterprises in the Indian hand-knitted carpet industry are small, marginal operations run by poor and illiterate men, and they have no margin to pay higher wages. Most of the employers have never attended school; they began weaving before age 14. An enterprise normally consists of a loom set-up in a family's one-room cottage, with perhaps an additional loom, or looms, in an attached veranda or a shed. Male family members, including children, provide the bulk of the labour.

India's Factories Act has influenced the current structure of the carpet industry. Costly health, safety and labour regulations to which large firms are subject do not apply to cottage industries. Only a small proportion of establishment has five or more looms.

Competition Limits Retail Price Increases

While child and adult weavers have similar productivity, there is a cost advantage to hiring child labour: children earn less while apprentices than do fully-trained weavers, and their addition to the workforce depresses the going wage rate. Replacing the 22 per cent of children in the workforce would likely cause the wage bill to rise by about 5 per cent.

Given the small scale of many weaving enterprises and the fact that weaving charges make up approximately 40 per cent of the total production cost, with the loom owner receiving a fee equivalent to 10 per cent of production costs for supervision and provision of looms and premises, it is clear that the use of child labour can add greatly to the revenues and profits of loom owners.

The extra labour costs involved in eliminating child labour become much easier to absorb further down the distribution chain. Importing country wholesalers mark up the carpets around 65 per cent, while foreign retailers typically mark up the carpets by approximately 200 per cent. With sales or value-added tax, the carpets can easily cost four times as much to the consumer as the Indian export price. This means that the overall savings in production costs from the use of child labour are very small when compared to the foreign retail price.

Finding solutions which satisfy both local weavers and foreign retailers must avoid a beggar-thy-neighbour spiral. If carpet producing countries simultaneously implemented a no-child-labour strategy in their hand-knitted carpet industries, none of them would be at a competitive disadvantage.

Methods of reducing child labour such as those used in the garment industry where there is tripartite collaboration to ensure that the children are treated well and that there are educational opportunities for them until they are replaced without economic hardship to their families, is not likely to work in the hand-knitted carpet industry. Neither labeling nor inspection is likely to work here because the industry is too fragmented. It is impossible to control the thousands of cottages where one or two carpets per year are woven. We need solutions that address the general problems of poverty while developing alternative source of both employment and education.

Child labour is not necessary in the carpet industry. Children do not possess a unique skill and there is a ready pool of surplus adult labour ready to take over from them. "People should not be fooled into thinking that child labour is necessary for the industry to survive. The irreplaceable skills or "nimble fingers" argument should no longer be used to justify the use of child labour in the carpet industry or any other industry.

20

Unemployment in the Poor and Rich Worlds

Different Causes, But Converging Policies?

In view of the magnitude of global unemployment, all the customary formulas offered by economists against mass unemployment—the basic socio-economic problem of modern times—appear to be quackery. Neither quantitative, nor any kin of 'qualitative', growth will be able to eliminate the disastrous worldwide lack of jobs. For ecological reasons it is impossible to include 800 million or more unemployed in the production process through corresponding growth. The resulting increase in global Gross Domestic Product would require consumption of natural resources, energy and the environment which, given even the greatest possible productivity in those sectors, could not even be sustained for two or three decades.

In addition, aiming to achieve full employment through growth will be even more difficult even in the rich economies. For it is most likely that work productivity will continue to rise worldwide. Countries such as China, which are in the initial phase of modernisation, are still producing at a relatively still low productivity rate. But that is precisely why they can achieve notable increases in productivity in a short time by importing technology from highly-developed countries. The advantage of rapid 'catch-up rationalisation', however, is being bought at the cost of rising unemployment and progressive impoverishment.

Employment Through Redistribution of Work

The notion that jobs can at some time be created for 800-900`million unemployed who will work 35 or even 40 hours a week at the productivity level of the highly-developed countries of four or five decades ago is absurd. The only realistic possibility of eliminating the world's unemployment problem is by far-reaching redistribution of work and income. The change needed for that demands fundamentally new concepts of prosperity: a reflection on the philosophy of the 'life of happiness'. 'New concepts of prosperity' means that technological progress would no longer be used mainly to deliver rising per capita incomes and excessive consumption. Instead, given a sufficient material standard of living, the quality of life would be improved primarily by shortening working hours. It is about, so to speak, assigning instrumental good sense new goals. Plus reshaping socio-economic conditions in such a way that the politicians will again be compelled to orient themselves on the good of the community and humanistic values instead of filling the pockets of the wealthy. It is sheer ideology, although very persuasive, to cite 'globalisation' and its alleged 'iron laws' in defaming the welfare state, full employment and social justice as out-of-date wishful thinking. A return to the state-guided social competitive system as practised during the first decades after the Second World War is possible just as it was politically feasible to make the transition from the old order of unfettered, ruthless capitalism to the mixed economies of the social market economy types. So it is a matter of restoring the proven structures of a mixed economic system.

However, in contrast to the first postwar decades it is now not sufficient to regenerate nation-sate interventionism. Appropriate international regualtions are required. Above all, it will depend upon reversing the new laissez-faire developments in international economic relationships which today are subsumed under the buzzword 'globalisation'. That is, to oppose over-liberalisation and its disastrous social and inhuman impacts. It will depend on the broad mobilisation of the losers in the process of globalisation whether the necessary fundamental change of course can still be made in time before a catastrophe. In particular, the new myth must be opposed that declares globalisation as a kind of law of nature and thus suggests resignation and adaptation to an allegedly unavoidable process of destruction of social and human achievements.

Mass Unemployment in the Poor Economies

The employment problems in the rich and the poor hemispheres differ not only in their magnitude, but also in their causes. The wretched condition of the poor economies is due above all to historical reasons: colonialism and, in the post-colonial era, the constraints to independent development imposed by the hegemonic influence of the rich industrial states. The waste of scarce resources by international and civil wars, and the dictatorships with their upperclass luxury consumption and inefficient, thus development—obstructing exploitation structures—often supported by the industrialised nations, have for a long time repressed and in many cases destroyed autonomous development potential. The colonial and post-colonial distortion also contributed at least indirectly to the current population problems of the poor countries. The politically inflicted mass poverty and under-development stabilised or in fact brought about economic, socio-psychological and ideological mechanisms which oppose an effective population policy. As we know, the average educational level in many developing countries, especially among women, is too low to give a modern population policy a chance of success. Mass unemployment in the poor countries is the result of poverty. In this respect, it is about a production-side problem: too few resources, to little real and human capital, and the inefficient, unproductive use of much of the anyway limited added value of society. The picture is totally different in the rich countries—the over-production economies.

Unemployment in Over-Production Systems

The main cause of mass unemployment in the industrialised nations has nothing to do with shortages. It is a phenomenon of surplus. Greater possibilities of production can no longer be used 'sufficiently profitably because the required demand is lacking. Production is done for profit. The necessary collateral condition is the satisfying of consumer needs. Employment is not even such a condition, but only a side effect which lapses immediately when labour-free production is technically possible. Thus, national income must be shared among wages and profits (or income from property). Profit is the difference between earnings and costs. Earnings depend upon demand. Macro-economic costs consist mainly of wages and salaries (including social security contributions). These definitive connections mean that profit can be made only if overall demand is greater than the total cost labour. But in the final analysis this demand can only come from the profit-earners themselves. In his book, a Treatise on Money, Keynes described this nexus as the theory of the Widow's cruse. Under capitalistic conditions, labour is only sought or hired if profit can be earned with it. But as making a profit depends upon the demand for consumption and investment by the shareholders, it can be seen that the degree of employment is determined by the demand behaviour of the class that receives income from property. In this respect, the widespread belief that greater investment also leads to more employment, namely via the effect of investment in demand, is right.

Lower Wages Mean Lower Demand

The lower the level of wages, and given an unchanged total demand, the greater are the profits that can be made. But it is more likely that in the case of falling wages the overall demand will also drop. For stabilising total demand would require the recipients of income from property to increase their spending on consumption and/or investment to the degree to which wages and the consumption based on them fell.

During the last 10 to 15 years the development of profits in most industrialised nations has been very favourable. But profits would have grown more strongly if the demand of the shareholder had been much greater. This would have created more employment at the same time. Thus, it can be assumed that the profits are simply too high for the shareholders to be able to go in for meaningful consumption or make profitable investments. That is the reason for the extreme redirection of capital from fixed assets to portfolio investment. The growth of speculative (unproductive) financial transactions during the 1980s and 1990s (buzzword: casino capitalism), corresponded with a relatively weak formation of real capital.

Wage rises, of course, narrows the scope for profit. But precisely this effect stimulated efforts to improve the profit situation not only by investment in rationalisation, but also by investment in expansion aimed at the growing mass purchasing power. Since more is being invested, the profit mass also is growing according to the principle of the widow's cruse. Too low wages, as it were, relieve the shareholders of the pressure to innovate and invest and allow them to earn their profits too easily. That is the real message of the 'purchasing power theory' of wages.

Over-accumulation and Under-consumption

Over-production has two different causes which, however, mostly occur in tandem. They are over-investment, or creation of over-capacities, on the one hand, and lack of demand due to relative saturation and an absence of mass purchasing power on the other. But the main reason for mass unemployment in the rich hemisphere currently lies on the demand side. During the first three decades after the Second World War supply and demand rose in relative balance. Economic fluctuations showed up as temporary declines in generally positive GDP growth rates. These decades of (dynamic) balance of growth are often described today as the era of 'Fordism'. Its essential feature is that rising wages ensure continuing growth of consumption, so that equally growing profits also flow relatively continuously into investments to expand capacity and create jobs. The label 'Fordism' expresses the 'simple' view of the theory for the buying power of wages which is said to have been propagated by Henry Ford I. This was that his workers should earn enough to be able to buy the cars they made.

The astonishingly balanced development of supply and demand from 1950 to the mid-1970s was due above all to postwar reconstruction and the pent-up demand of consumers who were starved by wartime economy shortages. This stimulated positive investment sentiment, and high investments brought at the same time high profits. The postwar growth that led within a short time to full employment was also linked with growth in productivity, which on multi-year average was more than twice that of the crisis period of the last 25 years. Thus, the so-called employment threshold (the GDP growth rate point at which employment growth begins) was much higher in those days than it is now, although there was full employment over a longer period. This simple fact opposes the thesis often propounded today that mass unemployment is above all related to rationalisation. It is not rationalisation per se, that is, progress that boosts productivity, which is the evil. The problem is that the mistakes in distribution policy which are rooted in capitalistic structures result in increases in supply encountering insufficient demand for goods, whereby the demand for labour drops. However, the fact that demand policy contradicts the requirements of a social ethic that is ecologically responsible and right for the interests of the poor countries was already spelled out. So if a demand-oriented growth policy is practised at all, it should be designed to be as environmentally compatible as possible. After all, there are possibilities for that, such as by expanding the production of services that spare resources. A one-hour driving lesson costs more energy than one hour of ballet instruction.

The politically initiated and implemented over-liberalisation and surrender of social prosperity to global competition since the 1970s, which reproduces the old self-destructive mechanism of laissez faire, have during the last two decades markedly accelerated the crisis development inherent in the system.

Summing up, It is Noted That

- Full employment in the rich economies would certainly be possible by means of demand policy, but only at a high cost to the environment that is concomitant with high growth rates;
- The growth policy of the rich countries impairs the poor economies' possibilities of medium to long-term growth, since these are falling back ever further in the competition for ever scarcer and thus ever more expensive resources;
- The environmental collapse currently expected for the third or fourth generation after us, which obviously also will trigger a collapse of the world economy and—probably ahead of that—armed conflicts which today are hardly imaginable, would happen very much sooner if economic growth were to be increased to such a degree that it would bring full employment worldwide;
- In the long term, the problem of global unemployment and global poverty can only be solved by a policy of massive redistribution, and in fact a redistribution of work and income, whereby increases in productivity must be used mainly or only for shortening working hours. That is a demand, which appears to be utopian. But utopias of today often have the quality of scripting the reality of tomorrow.

❑❑❑

21

Solving the Unemployment Problem by Looking Beyond the Job

If you had a job, you worked; if you didn't, you didn't. Having a job meant being employed by an organisation in a clearly-defined and stable occupational role, with duties, hours, rates of pay and promotion all more or less standardised. But the job—in that meaning of the world—is a social invention, and a fairly recent one.

The job—the kind that you had, or hoped to get—because a central fixture of life. Its importance was great because it served many needs: For managers and efficiency experts, job assignments were the key to assembly-line manufacturing. For union organizers, jobs protected the rights of workers. For political reformers, standardised civil service positions were the essence of good government. Jobs provided an identity the immigrants and recently-urbanised farm workers. They provided a sense of security for individuals and an organising principle for society.

Jobs functioned in so many ways that it is surprising how many organisations are now opting for other ways to define and manage work. The second job shift is underway. Its emergence can be seen in the increasing use of temporary and part-time workers and contracted-out services, the changing relationships between workers and management, the growing popularity of self-employment and small business. Indeed, "de-jobbing" is proceeding at such a pace that many economists, management experts and futurists are now taking freely about the end of the job. Bridges predicts that the job as we now know it will disappear entirely—replaced by new kinds of flexible work assignments in post-job organisations—and be remembered only as a quaint artifact of the industrial age.

One reason for the change in work is the economic rules of the survival game among organisations that employ workers. To stay successful in today's hi-tech consumer economy, business have had to re-model themselves into what some experts call "agile companies"—ones that are able to respond quickly to conditions in ever-changing, fragmenting, competitive markets.

The "knowledge worker", whose work involves not simply doing something, but also applying theoretical or analytical skills. Such workers are replacing the industrial labourer as the dominant part of the workforce—and their productive activities are likely to be organised and structured much differently from those of their assembly-line predecessors.

De-jobbing as a result of new technology or the emergence of a service economy is a phenomenon that gets a lot of attention these days; but it is not the whole story. At all levels of society, people are improvising livelihoods that do not fit the industrial-era model. Immigrants to the developed countries, often unable to find steady jobs, nevertheless find places in the new landscape by being mobile, flexible, resourceful and imaginative: they moonlight, work part-time, share jobs, start small businesses. Their lives are often extremely difficult, but they are also instructive to those of us who believe you either have a job or you're out of luck.

It is too early to evaluate the implications of this multifaceted transformation of work, or to dismiss it as simply good or bad. Nevertheless, one cannot deny that it is taking place, and will bring about dramatic social changes.

On the downside, the job shift is causing great hardships for many workers and their families. It poses serious challenges to policy-makers, political activists and labour leaders. The basic question appears to be whether the key to global employment-development strategy is to play "catch-up"—trying to bring millions of people around the world into jobs in industries and the public sector, or to play "leapfrog"—creating new forms of employment.

The proposal to generate more employment in agriculture, for example, is based on new demand for agricultural exports from developing countries. The policies designed to make the most of this opportunity include measures to upgrade technology, raise productivity, ensure the supply of essential inputs, establish marketing and distribution channels, create links between agriculture and industry, and cater to export markets.

The issue of part-time work, another kind of employment that is seriously undervalued in the traditional industrial era job mind-set. Part-time work may not offer much at this point to developing countries, where many people are under employed and wages are low, but it can be of great help in more advanced economies. And it is likely to be a big part of the global work picture in the years ahead.

A certain agility may also be necessary in agriculture, particularly in countries that for many years have depended heavily on producing commodities such as sugar for export as a means of generating income and employment. As Northern laboratories develop non-agricultural substitutes for many of these commodities—and this is already beginning to happen—the bottom may fall out of "monoculture" economies, only economic, but will have long-run political implications as communities attempt to reorganize themselves in response to the changed conditions. It is, therefore, in the interest of raw materials exporters to closely monitor current trends in biotechnology and the use of genetic resources and modify their internal policies in anticipation of potential long-term effects.

This calls for flexibility, and an ability to get information and to act on it. Government officials, development workers, community leaders and individuals will, in some respects, all have to be "knowledge workers" if they are to keep ahead of global changes. Jobs are going to be created not just by putting people to work, but by finding—or creating—new niches where they can be productive.

It is still possible to talk about jobs for all, and to resist the assumption made by many economists that high levels of unemployment are now inevitable. But, as we move ahead into the global information economy, we may be moving back into an older conception of the job, and seeing it again as something you do, rather than as something you have—or that has you.

❑❑❑

22

Employment and Poverty Alleviation

Today the key socio-economic problem is large-scale unemployment. Spreading joblessness brings many other problems in its wake. It erodes national incomes and living standards, aggravating the already grindingly difficult job of promoting development and alleviating poverty. Joblessness also raises government budget deficits, increasing macro-economic instability while soaking up investment for productive capital expenditure, education, training and relief aid. And joblessness ruins lives and communities by depriving people of the dignity and satisfaction that comes with earning one's keep and making a contribution to the well-being of family and society.

Theories about how best to nurture development (and thus create jobs) have shifted considerably over the last decade. The state role has evolved, in the minds of many, from being a source of relief for the problems of unemployment, poverty and underdevelopment, to being a fundamental cause of these problems through the distorting impact of its intervention on the market.

However, the more market-oriented philosophy that grew up during the 1990s has yet to provide convincing solutions in practice at least not on a grand scale and especially not in terms of job creation as the present jobless economic recovery demonstrates.

The weakness of the current recovery and past approaches to economic development can be traced to the failure to consider employment as the predominant means of promoting growth and alleviating poverty. In policy circles it has too long been an almost ignored priority.

Current trends thus bode poorly, particularly as unemployment rates soar. In light of the circumstances, we need to begin re-examining some of the fundamental questions—if only to find out what has gone wrong with the answers.

Minimum Wage?

Let's begin with wages. With corporate restructuring in full force on a global scale, are low wage rates required to raise employment and maximize profits? A top manager of a multinational consumer electronics group certainly thinks so; he likened the perfect factory to a ship "so that we could move it around the world to where labour was cheapest". Perhaps, but this bottom-line emphasis on unit labour costs ignores at least two other factors; namely, that higher wages can act as a screen to select more productive workers and that higher wages translate into better productivity via improved worker nutrition, increased consumption and a generally healthier quality of life.

If higher wages bring these benefits (and it is an open question) should government insist that there be a minimum wage rate? Neo-classical economists tend to respond "no", assuming that a higher wage rate puts money into the pockets of some low wage workers while forcing many others out of work because companies cannot afford to pay them.

Technology Transfer

The impact of technology is another area in need of study. Technological innovation is usually labour-saving and tends to originate in industrialized countries, moving toward developing countries like India, Pakistan where labour tends to be low cost and abundant. Would it therefore make sense to slow down or somehow restrict technology transfer, especially to development markets, in the interest of preserving employment?

The answer here is clearly—no, historical evidence abundantly demonstrates that attempts to retard technological progress bring about greater poverty and lower growth. Technology, infact, is at the heart of the new endogenous growth theory which is very much in vogue among development economists today. Slowing down or inhibiting technology transfer would certainly dash many countries' development hopes and aggravate poverty. However, the relationship between technology, development, employment and poverty alleviation is not without its complications.

In the 1980s, the buzz word among development specialists was "appropriate technology", i.e., small-scale and labour-intensive technologies that would increase productive output while allowing an equilibrium solution to be found such that the ratio of the productivity of labour to that of capital is proportional to their relative prices. The conditions for this "small is beautiful" approach to technology tended to be best met in agricultural production. However, where manufacturing industry is concerned, the small-is-beautiful approach foundered badly when the only viable technological alternatives proved to be highly capital-intensive.

Development Gap

A wide gap has emerged between developing countries with an inward focus (which tended to be protectionist and pursue policies of import substitution) and those with an outward focus and a policy of pursuing export-led growth. Competing in international markets requires technology that is as good as or better than that found in advanced, industrialized nations. Small, therefore, is not beautiful in the global manufacturing economy where product standards are high and the elasticity of substitution between labour and capital is very limited.

The drive to obtain state-of-the-art technology thus leads to a policy conundrum: it is a pre-condition for success in manufactured exports, but the impulse to compete successfully in this most lucrative sector speeds up the transfer of technology from the developed to the developing world, thus reinforcing the bias toward labour saving equipment in developing countries and accelerating a process that is seen as a source of job loss in the industrialized countries.

Technology and Jobs

Before concluding that modern technology transfer is inimical to employment in developing countries, we have to distinguish clearly between technology's static and dynamic consequences. In a static sense, it is true that highly capital-intensive export industries may not create much employment on a net basis, but the dynamic effects of technology transfer do contribute to economic growth. And growth, in turn, generates multiplier effects in the form of demand, which stimulates ancillary production activities (like food processing or consumer goods) that rely on more labour-intensive technologies.

The problem is that the diffusion and application of technology on a global scale blurs the categories of international product specialisation and creates a much more competitive and conflict-prone international environment.

For example, we have already seen the Asian Tigers move from producing goods such as textiles and processed food to producing hi-tech and value-added consumer durables. This advance is only possible due to the growth of human capital (facilitated by investment and higher incomes) and it leaves production of textiles to other industrializing countries, like Indonesia, the Philippines and now China. But the dynamic comes at the expense of jobs in industrialized regions, like the US and the EC, which lost more than a quarter of their work force in textiles during the 1980s. In spite of job losses, advanced countries continue to produce textiles, notwithstanding major differences in the hourly wage rates for spinning and weaving and the fact that essentially the same hi-tech equipment is being used in most production centres.

Protectionism

What has happened in textiles is happening in other industrial sectors (automobiles, for example) as well. The intense market competition is proving to be a source of trade conflicts, and possibly protectionism, as jobs come under increasing pressure.

For many workers and managers, the benefits of foreign direct investment look increasingly like a zero-sum game for employment, and there is a real risk that the tenuous link between overall growth and employment will break down altogether. It is hardly surprising that we are already seeing negatively affected workers and local businesses clamouring for protection in advanced countries.

Governments Role

The concerned governments are suppose to carry out much of this research. The three initial lines of inquiry follow from three reasonable assumptions about the future.

- First, increase in welfare and consumption subsidies are out; investments in training and human capital are in. How can investments in human capital be directed to positive employment effects? Is it perhaps not time to explore more fully benefit schemes targeting the unemployed and the unskilled poor providing them with the type of subsidies that would enhance their human capital, improve their health and productivity through better nutrition and preventive medicine, and restore the dignity of holding a job?
- Second, given the quasi-inevitability of increased automation in manufacturing, how can other sectors (particularly agriculture and services) be developed to

export their long-term potential for employment creation?

- Third, given the inevitable pressures of work and productivity in the global economy, what sort of alternative institutional arrangements need to evolve with respect to industrial relations, employment and work conditions?

Finding answers to these and other questions will require no small amount of new thinking, but parochialism or a failure of imagination would be fatal flaws in this global era.

23

Trade and Labour Standards

Using the Wrong Instruments for the Right Cause

A moral value is a shared concern of humanity; hence its enforcement should be a cooperative task implemented for the benefit of humankind. Would we qualify recent approaches to the issue of trade and labour standards as non-inquisitory but shared and cooperatives ones? The purpose of this brief is to shed some light on this question.

In fact, nobody, will deny any country the right to raise and fight for issues which are of moral concern for humanity, as they are supposed to benefit humankind. The issue of implementing and enforcing a core of labour standards one of these.

However, a problem remains: who has the negotiating power to raise and impose them? The key issue is that trade coercive attempts by some become inquisitorial as soon as they are backed by moral concerns which are supposed to be shared by all, while the same "all" lack the negotiating power to be, in turn, coercive if they so wish. In other words, trade related coercion forcedly becomes "inquisition" when moral concerns are introduced into the functioning of an international trading system characterised by large imbalances in the negotiating power of the participating countries. Only a few Governments have the negotiating leverage and strength to develop what we may qualify as "trade-related inquisitory practices".

The issue of trade and labour standards seems to have arisen when "uniform competition" has been regarded as a threat to employment and economic growth in some industrial countries.

However, without attaining a certain degree of international agreement and coherence as to whether and under what conditions—a given competitive advantage is, or is not, related to social or other conditions, and whether or not it may, be considered as "unfair". With protectionist views in mind, such an approach may only be interpreted as "unbenign thinking" coming from "unfair competitiveness seekers".

If the motivation behind the introduction and further use of moral argumentation is to seek a justification for the possible use of trade measures as enforcement mechanisms to achieve certain goals. Particularly for harmonisation of labour standards, one may wonder why the labour standards issue has not been linked to North-North trade in the current debate on the considerable variation in labour standards among developed countries. The motivation may well be that in the post-Uruguay Round era, when tariffs have been reduced substantially and "grey area measures" put under stricter control or even banned, we may be facing the possible revival of new forms of protectionism wearing "blue", "green" or "multicolour" masks. On the contrary, if the motivation behind the introduction of such moral labour rights argumentation reflects a real commitment by the international community to enforce labour standards, a door may be open for embarking, in the future, on a series on international initiatives, not necessarily under the trade umbrella.

It should also be stressed that the linkage between trade and labour standards has been seriously misinterpreted. Most analysts remain blind to the two-way character of the link between trade and labour standards. On the one hand, trade liberalisation is to promote growth and development by promoting a more efficient allocation of resources and to ease the adoption and implementation of labour standards, as well as to promote job creation. On the other hand—and this is extremely important raising labour standards—not keeping them low—should increasingly be seen as the real source of competitiveness and economic growth through, among others, increase in the quality of labour. There is a case for considering economic progress and the rise in labour standards as mutually reinforcing.

Turning to the low labour standards debate, much more empirical and analytical evidence is needed to asses the extent to which low labour standards are correlated to lower wages and labour costs. Although raising labour standards may not primarily be intended to maximise efficiency, it is becoming increasingly evident that efficiency and the future potential of the firm may not necessarily be maximised by keeping labour standards low. In this context, it is the development to human capital in LDCs which is a top priority, not because failing to respect labour standards in these economies threatens the welfare of the workers in the industrialised countries but, more simply, because it is the only strategy for enhancing the productivity of labour and ultimately increasing the people's standard of living. Thus, if raising labour standards and ensuring their effective implementation is important for economic progress, developed and developing countries, as well as wokers and employers in each region, should adopt a cooperative, not confrontational approach in order to deal with this urgent and pressing problem. For this very reason, adherence to trade sanctions would be a wrong approach. Trade is essential for enhancing woker's productivity because it ensures that a country's resources will be employed in the activities that it is best at. In turn, increased productivity is the key to development, higher labour standards and higher wages. Moreover, the issue of labour standards is of a moral nature: it has an undeniable development dimension which needs to be more clearly perceived but, as discussed, it is certainly not an issue to be dealt with through trade measures.

Labour standards should be dealt with in the WTO. The capacities of the ILO will prove invaluable for renewed multilateral effort to improve working conditions in developing countries. Its tripartite structure has proved to be the best suited to the tasks of conciliation and dialogue.

Improving the standards of living and labour standards for workers or eradicating child labour is what matters it is the right cause for humankind, a cause to fight for, through various approaches and by using all the mechanisms at our disposal in order to ensure its success. Thus, the issue is not one of trade and labour standards, but of labour standards and economic development, an issue of a human dignity and human rights nature. It is a universal issue, the solutions to which should be found by all nations, taking into account equity considerations. Each country should participate in the process, depending on its level of economic development. It is precisely because economic development, including trade, is positively correlated with the adoption and effective implementation of labour standards that solutions to low labour standards should not necessarily come from negative and coercive approaches. Solutions for universal problems must not only be efficiency-based but also equity-based. Therefore, the case is for cooperation rather than coercion and for applying positive instruments. As in the case of environmental issues, developing countries should be recipients of funds, technical cooperation and other similar forms of support when the implementation of labour standards involves an inequitable cost burden.

The initiative of "grouping" a core of existing conventions into a new global convention on core labour standards of universal value may, in view of its new and distant qualitative nature, generate strong support from the international community for its implementation. The ILO was created to promote workers' right, so the initiative could be launched under its aegis, in direct collaboration with other intergovernmental organisations dealing with social, trade and development issues in an interrelated manner. The support to this or other similar approaches by the international community, and in particular by those developed countries that have recently shown a special and strong interest in the reinforcement and implementation of labour rights in developing countries, will be a clear sign of their dergree of sincerity and their willingness to share the social concerns of universal value which seem to be of paramount interest to most of their citizens.

24

Population Growth and Jobs

Since mid-century, the world's labour force has more than doubled, from 1.2 billion people to 2.7 billion, outstripping the growth in job creation. As a result, the United Nations International Labour Organisation estimates that nearly 1 billion people, approximately 30 per cent of the global work force, are unemployed or underemployed (working but not earning enough to meet basic needs). Over the next half-century, the world will need to create more than 1.9 billion jobs—all of them in the developing world—just to maintain current levels of employment.

As economists often note, while population growth may boost labour demand (through economic activity and demand for goods), it will most definitely boost labour supply. During the next 50 years, almost 40 million people will enter the global labour force—defined as those between the ages of 15 and 65 seeking work—each year. Between 1995 and 2050, some 1.9 billion additional jobs will need to be created to absorb these new would-be workers. The most pressing needs will be found in the world's poorest nations—a sobering example of the vicious cycle linking poverty and population growth.

As the children of today represent the workers of tomorrow, the interaction between population growth and jobs is most acute in nations with young populations. Nations such as Peru, Mexico, Indonesia, and Zambia with more than half their population below the age of 25 will feel the burden of this labour flood. In the Middle East and Africa, 40 per cent of the population is under the age of 15. Since new entrants into the labour force were born at least 15 years ago, measures to reduce population growth have a delayed effect on the growth of the labour force, highlighting the urgency of taking action on population.

Nowhere is the employment challenge greater than in Africa, where at least 40 per cent of the population lives in absolute poverty. Although 8 million people entered the sub-Saharan work force in 1997, by 2030 this resource-scarce region will have to absorb more than 17 million new entrants each year. Over the next half-century, Nigeria's labour force is projected to grow by 246 per cent and Ethiopia's will soar by 337 per cent—both faster than growth of the general population. At current growth rates, the size of the labour force in sub-Saharan Africa will more than triple by 2050.

As a result of unprecedented population growth and increasing acceptance of female participation in the work force, the number of people seeking jobs in the Middle East and North Africa, a region already plagued by double-digit unemployment rates, will double in the next 50 years. In Algeria, where unemployment stands at 22 per cent, the labour force is growing at a staggering 4.2 per cent annually, and the number seeking work will more than double by 2050. Egypt alone will need to create 26 million more jobs by 2050 as its total population hits 115 million.

Nations throughout Asia will also see phenomenal increases in the numbers seeking work, including Pakistan, where the work force will grow from 70 million in 1998 to 205 million by 2050. Over the next 25 years, India will add nearly 10 million to its work force each year. During the same period, China will add nearly 6 million annually due to population growth alone, compounding the work shortages caused by the current flood of migrants to China's coastal cities and by massive layoffs—estimated at more than 30 million—as state-run operations are scaled back.

Nations are hard-pressed to educate and train rapidly growing numbers of young people in marketable skills for the global workplace. Moreover, meeting the basic needs of a growing population draws scarce foreign exchange and other resources from investments in education and job creation. Throughout the world, young people entering the work force are increasingly faced with unemployment and social marginalisation. In most societies, unemployment rates for those under 25 are substantially higher than for older people.

Surplus farmland once served as a traditional source of employment for growing populations, as new land could be ploughed to generate work and income. However, global per capita Greenland has dropped by half and considerably more in certain nations since 1950. Moreover, the mechanisation of agriculture fuels the exodus of job seekers into the world's urban areas, where unemployment is often most acute, heavily reliant on natural capital in the past, future job creation will require massive amounts of financial capital to jump-start the industrial and service sectors.

As the balance between the demand and supply of labour is tipped by population growth, wages—the price of labour—tend to decrease. And in a situation of labour surplus, the quality of jobs may not improve as fast for workers will settle for longer hours, fewer benefits and less control over work activities.

Employment is the key to obtaining food, housing, health services, and education, in addition to providing self-respect and self-fulfilment. Rising numbers of unemployed people could drive global poverty and hunger to precarious levels, fueling political instability.

25

The WTO is Born

Affirming that "the establishment of the World Trade Organisation (WTO) ushers in a new era of global economic cooperation, reflecting the widespread desire to operate in a fairer and more open multilateral trading system for the benefit and welfare of their people," more than a hundred ministers in the ancient trading crossroads of Marrakesh signed the Final Act of the Uruguay Round and made decisions ensuring a running start for the WTO.

In the ornate Salle Royale of the Palaisdes Congress, the ministers, one by one, signed. The Final Act containing 28 agreements and appended to by some 26,000 pages of national tariff and services schedules, which GATT economists estimate will add some US $ 755 billion to world exports and raise incomes by some $ 235 billion annually.

Several ministers also signed the new Government Procurement Code that was negotiated in parallel with the Uruguay Round and three other plurilateral agreements: on dairy products, bovine meat and civil aircraft. The ceremony effectively marked the start of the transition from GATT to the WTO.

In the Marrakesh Declaration they had adopted just hours earlier, the Ministers had saluted as "a historic achievement" the conclusion of the round, which strengthen the world economy, lead to more trade, investment, employment and income growth throughout the world". They had also expressed their determination to "resist protectionist pressures of all kinds". In this regard, they pledged, with immediate effect and until the establishment of the WTO, not to "take any trade measures that would undermine or adversely affect the results of the Uruguay Round negotiations or their implementation."

Ministerial Decisions

The establishment of a Preparatory Committee for the WTO was one of the four decisions taken by ministers. The other three were: the Decision on Acceptance of and Accession to the Agreement Establishing the World Trade Organisation; the Decision on Trade and Environment; and the Decision on Organisational and Financial Consequences flowing from Implementation of the Agreement Establishing the WTO.

The Preparatory Committee, to be headed by Mr. Peter Sutherland in his personal capacity, will be in charge of ensuring an orderly transition from the GATT to the WTO. Its remit is to ensure the efficient operation of the WTO immediately as of the date of its establishment. Thus, it will convene and prepare the Implementation Conference, which will decide formally on the date of entry into force of the WTO Agreement.

Opening Ceremonies

"Our meeting here in Marrakesh takes place at the close of the most ambitious trade negotiations in world economic history—we should be proud of this stride towards a more open world which will be, through the dynamism of exchanges between nations and the lifting of barriers and protectionist regulations, a source of prosperity and welfare for the people worldwide," said His Royal Highness the Crown Prince Sidi Mohammed at the opening of the Ministerial Meeting. He stressed that "we all are witnessing here in Marrakesh what will be the legal and institutional pillar of International Trade in the twenty–first century."

The TNC Chairman at Ministerial level, Minister Sergio Abreau Bonilla (Uruguay), opened the Ministerial Meeting by reminding participants that the real effectiveness of the new trade rules depended on the political will of governments. "We must therefore strengthen our determination to honour the commitments which we will assume with the signature of the Final Act," he said. Minister Abreau added: "Behind each signature, there are millions of workers, farmers, industrialists, professionals and businessmen who harbour the hope that the results of the Round will create new horizons for trade, employment and investment and offer better possibilities of tackling poverty and recession, paving the way for the economic and social development of nations."

Sutherland's Report

"Few trading caravans can have viewed this beautiful city with as much pleasure and as much relief—as ours does. But then very few trading caravans were on the road for more than seven years, and none carried such a priceless cargo. This week you as Ministers will sign the greatest trade agreement in history, one whose benefits span entire continents and a wide range of trade sectors alike," the TNC Chairman at Officials Level, GATT Director-General Peter Sutherland said.

Mr. Sutherland reported that the work of the TNC since the successful conclusion of the Uruguay Round negotiations on 15 December 1993 had been focused on the preparations for the Marrakesh Meeting. First, the Final Act Embodying the Results of the Uruguay Round of Multilateral Trade Negotiations was legally rectified, agreed and circulated to all participants. Secondly, the schedules of market access commitments in goods and services and the MFN exemption lists in services were multilaterally verified for attachment to the Marrakesh Protocol. Thus the Final Act, rectified and completed by the verified schedules, was now well as trade and investment.

Reflecting on the successful conclusion of the negations, US Trade Representative Michael Kantor said he was "struck by the thin line that separates success and failure... (but) we succeeded because the ties that bind us together are stronger than the forces seeking to pull us apart." He stressed that "our vision of the trading system must be dynamic and able to meet the emerging challenges to our collective global economic growth." Thus, "increasingly, we will address issues related to each other's internal policies, such as competition policy and other domestic regulatory policies, as well as environmental protection and labour standards."

Canada's Trade Minister, Mr. Roy MacLaren, emphasised that when WTO is asked to tackle new trade policy issues, it should proceed in a manner consistent with its competence and mandate. He warned that "when examining new issues, we must, for example be wary of being seduced by the argument that differing approaches to issues such as environmental protection constitute an unfair trade practice justifying some form of action—new issues can become a vehicle for new protectionism." Minister MacLaren stressed that "to fall victim in the World Trade Organisation to the narrow interest groups who favour trade sanctions as the instrument of choice to force nations to comply with the policies of other would be to abandon some of the most fundamental gains we have made."

Development Goals

India's Minister of Commerce, Mr. Pranab Mukherjee, warned that the acute differences between levels of development and incomes among nations have "enough latent heat to melt down the most elaborately engineered structures." Thus, "the long-term survival of the multilateral trading system will depend upon reducing the present inequities." Regarding new issues, Minister Mukherjee said while India was strongly committed to internationally-recognised labour standards, it could not see any merit in linking this subject to international trade. On the other hand, he attached importance to an examination in the Preparatory Committee of the relationship between immigration policies and international trade.

Bangladesh's Minister for Commerce, Mr. M. Shamsul Islam, speaking on behalf of the least-developed countries, hoped that "in the implementation of the Uruguay Round Agreements, the international community will be more responsive to the needs of the most disadvantaged group of nations." He urged a comprehensive assessment of the Uruguay Round results with "any imbalances...to be redressed through appropriate action including additional trade preferences, development assistance and debt relief." Minister Islam pointed to the "need by LLDCS for substantial technical assistance in the implementation of the results of the Round. On new issues, he supported the consideration of the relationship between movements of natural persons and international trade in the Preparatory Committee.

Zimbabwe's Minister of Industry and Commerce, Dr. H. Murerwa, said that his country's preliminary evaluation of the Uruguay Round results suggested gains for certain products, stand–still position for others and potential losses for some products as a result of erosion of EC trade preferences. However, he believed that "the process of liberalisation will in the long–run strengthen the global trading system and benefit the peoples of both the developed and developing countries." Minister Murerwa said the challenge facing the developing countries is "to expand and diversify our export capabilities as well as strengthening the international competitiveness of our products." Reready for signature by Ministers. Simultaneously, the TNC at official level had approved for adoption by Ministers four decisions and Marrakesh Declaration.

The GATT Director-General said that "the signature ceremony will be a just cause for celebration not only because it represents signing-off on the Uruguay Round, but because it will be signing-on to the work of putting the results into effect and ensuring that their potential is used to the fullest."

Early Ratification Urged

Many Ministers underlined the urgency of ratifying the Uruguay Round agreements to enable the World Trade Organisation to be fully operational.

EC Commissioner Sir Leon Brittan emphasised that: "each of us, by our signature at Marrakesh, pledges himself or herself to submit the results of the Uruguay Round for formal approval in accordance with our domestic laws and, equally important, to proceed without delay to implement in our domestic laws, the commitments we made during the negotiations" He said one proof of the quality of those commitments was "the ever-lengthening queue of candidates for accession to the GATT and to the WTO." The EC Commissioner suggested that the WTO tackle the following issues: ensuring intensive cooperation between the WTO and the IMF and the World Bank; addressing urgently the interface between trade and the environment; working with the International Labour Office and other organisations, the WTO must address problems such as child exploitation, forced labour or the denial to workers of free speech or free association; and distortion of trade which can be caused by different standards of competition law and practice in different countries.

Japan's Deputy Prime Minister and Minister for Foreign Affairs Mr. Tsutomu Hata, underlined the importance of the Round's conclusion "in securing confidence in the world economic order." He recalled that his country had made significant contributions to the Round, including acceptance of the Agreement on Agriculture and cutting average tariffs on industrial and mining products by 61 per cent to rate as low as 1.5 per cent. "As a result of the Uruguay Round, the Japanese market offers greater opportunities for success by foreign exporters depending upon their efforts," he added. Minister Hata expressed strong support for the early entry into force of the WTO Agreement, and suggested that the WTO consider additional issues closely related to trade, including regionalism as grading the WTO, he viewed "Marrakesh as the stating platform which will put in place a strong rule-based multilateral trading system that should safeguard the interest of all nations, weak and strong."

The Swiss Minister of Public Economy, Mr. J. P. Delamuraz, pointed out that "by concluding the Uruguay Round, we have taken a decisive step towards the adaptation of the multilateral trading system to contemporary economic realities." This had meant for many participants "substantial adjustments" in domestic economic policy, and for Switzerland reforms in its agricultural policy. "We have added a number of stones to the foundations of a system of multilateral management of the world economy," said Mr. Delamuraz, "we have also recognise the interdependence that is binding us ever more closely together." He noted with special satisfaction the confirmation in the Marrakesh Declaration of the "need for positive measures on behalf of the developing countries, and especially of the least developed among them, as well as the desirability of possible additional measures for their benefit." Mexico's Secretary for Trade and Industrial Development, Mr. Jaime Serra Puche, lauded the result of the Round as signifying "recognition" of the adjustment measures that have been taken up by many developing countries to open their economies. He believed that the results "will further the creation of new jobs and growth in the wage levels of our workers." Secretary Puche stressed that "protection of the environment and workers' rights must go hand in hand with efforts to liberalise world trade, for progress in liberalisation to improve the environment and the well-being of workers," but warned against these subject being used as pretexts for "desguised trade protectionism."

Brazil's Minister of External Relations, Mr. Celso Amorium, said that the Uruguay Round "will be remembered as the first one in which developing countries had an active participation in the course of the whole negotiating process." He underlined that "We, the developing countries, have bet on trade liberalisation and on the multilateral trading system... . Even though our organisation does not bear the word development in its name, it will lose much of its purpose if its rules and disciplines do not contribute to freeing hundreds of millions of human beings from poverty and misery."

The Czech Republic's Minister of Industry and Trade, Mr. Vladimir Dlouhy, highlighted the importance his country attached to "the full integration of the economies in transition into the multilateral trading system." Pointing to these countries' need for better access to markets and fair application of trade and competition rules, he urged that "the role of the multiateral trading system in this process should be made more effective and more visible."

Singapore's Minister for Trade and Industry, Mr. Yeo Cheow Tong, said "the signing of the Final Act does not mean the end...the challenge now is to see through the successful establishment of the WTO and the implementation of the agreement." Minister Yeo said that Singapore fully supported the WTO because it "has long recognised that the free market system is way to economic growth and prosperity for our people." In line with this, he extended his country's invitation to host the first Ministerial Meeting of the WTO. "This will be the first time a major global trade meeting will be held in Asia, and will complete the circle of Uruguay Round meetings that began in South America in Uruguay, then moved on the North America, to Europe and today in Marrakesh, Africa," he added.

Conclusion

At the conclusion of the Ministerial Meeting, Minister Abreau noted that many of the one hundred ministers who have spoken had stressed that "notwithstanding the tumultuous economic and political events of the past seven-

and-a-half years, all participants have undertaken considerable efforts to improve conditions of market access." Noteworthy too had been "the engagement of the developing and least-developed countries in the process of countributing their share to the global effort to reduce trade barriers."

Another major theme was "the role that multilateral cooperation must play as the foundation for trade relations amongst nations." Min. Abreau said that to implement this principle on a permanent basis, "all had agreed that the results of the negotiations constituted a single undertaking, based on the WTO as a new international institution." He added that one decision taken at the meeting was the convening of an Implementation Conference later in the year.

In the course of the meeting, the TNC Chairman said ministries had stressed the importance they attached to the examination in the Preparatory Committee of the following subjects for inclusion in the WTO agenda: the relationship between the trading system and internationally recognised labour standards; the relationship between immigration policies and international trade; trade and competition policy, including rules on export financing and restrictive business practices; trade and investment; regionalism; the interaction between trade policies and policies relating to financial and monetary matters, including debt and commodity markets; international trade and company law; the establishment of a mechanism for compensation for the erosion of preferences; the link between trade, development, political stability and the alleviation of poverty; and unilateral or extraterritorial trade measures.

26

World Trade—The Next Challenge

On 15 December 1993 the world changed. My be not as dramatically as the moment when the Berlin Wall fell, but then unlike that very necessary demolition job, the success of the Uruguay Round was a work of construction. Like the destruction of the wall, though, its effects will be profound and lasting ones felt far beyond its immediate context. It will be seen as a defining moment in modern history.

The importance of the Round can be seen in terms of boost it gives to job creation; to development; to investment; to economic reform; to the rule of law and in many other ways besides. All of these benefits are real and important. But the true value of the whole is much, much more than the sum of these parts.

Put simply, governments came to the conclusion that the notion of a new world order was not merely attractive but absolutely vital; that the reality of the global market–whatever ambitions some of them may retain for regional integration—required a level of multilateral cooperation never before attempted.

No Losers in the Round

It has created a revolutionary framework for economic, legal and political cooperation. But now turn to the immediate results of the Round. Seeing them as a profit and loss account or a scorecard of winners and losers is to see them in static terms, as one-off conclusions with finite effects. This misses the point completely.

Every nation now needs an effective trading system, but especially so the small and poor. They have it. Everyone will also gain from the huge package of market access results even if they did not get every concession they were seeking from trading partners—it is the biggest market access deal ever negotiated.

However, the essence of the Uruguay Round's achievements is that they are dynamic. The new agreements, the new rules and structures it sets up—all mean a commitment to a continuing process of cooperation and reform of which the agreement in December was only the beginning.

Maintaining the liberalising momentum will call for continuing effort and vigilance by participating countries. But now their energy can be focused through the Round's greatest innovation; the new World Trade Organisation (WTO) in place of the improvised basis on which the GATT has operated for 45 years, trade will now have a permanent forum appropriate to its importance in the world economy.

Technically speaking, the WTO will oversee the implementation of the Round's results, administer all the agreements in goods, services and intellectual property, and manage the unified dispute settlement system. But beyond these administrative functions, it will raise the political profile of trade which has already been lifted greatly by the Uruguay Round. The WTO will have regular instead of occasional—direct Ministerial involvement. It will have a clear mandate to act as a forum for further trade negotiations. Most of all it will complete the transition from a trading system which largely restricted itself to policies at the border to one which also covers most aspects of domestic policy-making affecting international competition in goods and services, as well as investment.

Through the WTO, the Round will change the way the world economy is shaped. But it is not the final victory over protectionism and unilateralism. Any premature rejoicing would have quickly been cut short by the evidence since 15

December that major economic powers are still ready to take the unilateral approach to trade problems. Arguments for protectionism based on the alleged threat of low-cost competition to production and jobs will not just fade away because the Round is a success. The seductive appeal of "beggar-thy-neighbour" policies is highlighted by the seemingly greater vigour of the lobbies for protectionism than the advocates of open markets.

These dangers—and the speed with which they have resurfaced—make the achievement of the Uruguay Round all the more important, and its successful implementation all the more urgent. Implementation requires more than mutual backslapping about what we have achieved. It requires now that the US, EU and Japan, in particular, rapidly obtain final authority to ratify and also take a lead in providing the WTO with the means to fulfil its mandate.

The success of the Round has come at a time when it is even more vitally needed than anyone could have guessed when it was launched in 1986. Old structures and alignments have been turned inside out in trade as in every other area of international relations. We face a world of change and challenge, in which the reinforced trading system will be a primary source of stability and security.

The developing countries including India have become enthusiastic supporters of the multilateral trading system and the Uruguay Round even if all their demands were not met by industrial countries. The reasons lie in the changing economic policies of many developing countries and the clearer appreciation of the value of the GATT system that has grown along with these changes.

The challenge of new issues in world trade will be a major one for the WTO. The new organisation has to consider issues such as the links between trade and the environment, international competition policy, trade and investment, and trade and labour standards. To say a few words about trade and the environment since it is one area in which GATT member countries have committed themselves already to a comprehensive new work programme. They decided on 15 December, in conjunction with the adoption of the results of the Uruguay Round negotiations, to draw up a work programme on trade and environment by the Ministerial meeting in Marrakesh. Environmental policy-making is one of the most rapidly evolving areas of national and international policy-making, and it is entirely appropriate that emphasis should be placed now in GATT/WTO on ensuring better policy coordination and multilateral cooperation over the linkages between trade and environment.

Permanent Negotiations

The Uruguay Round may well be the last of its kind, but this in no way means the end of multilateral trade negotiations. On the contrary, it means they become a permanent event. Ad hoc negotiating rounds were necessary mainly because the GATT lacked the mandate or the institutional basis to operate the multilateral system to the full on a continuous basis. Between rounds the GATT has tended to lose momentum, often at the very times when it was essential to make the most of the liberalising impulse. This has allowed protectionism and unilateralism to recover and regroup and meant that each round has to start by regaining lost ground.

The positive results of the Uruguay Round will redefine much more than assumptions about trade. If they are exploited with the same determination, courage and commitment that went into concluding the Round, they should mean nothing less than a new start for sustainable growth and a new system of collective economic security for the world.

But if the trading system is now up to the job of supporting multilateral cooperation on such a wide scale, do the other structures of economic cooperation still meet the bill? The establishment of the WTO will put trade and investment on a par—perhaps rather in advance—of cooperation in monetary and financial areas. The WTO will stand alongside its original Bretton Woods sisters, the IMF and the World Bank. The three institutions must learn to work together even more effectively and closely. For example, rather than each body conducting separate reviews of country policies, is there not a case to be made for a more integrated approach on country reviews? But that does not, on its own, add up to effective multilateral economic cooperation. The question really has to be asked seriously: are the G7, the OECD, the regional groupings adequate to provide that cooperation?

It is the next challenge of international economic leadership—the challenge of translating the common interest in global growth into a practical and effective mechanism for solving our common economic problems together. So, the Ministers meeting in Marrakesh is an historic event which will establish the World Trade Organisation and put in place the new multilateral trading system, they will be making not an end, but a beginning.

27

Consuming the Future

Now that we are to reach six billion of us, it is a good point to check again on what sort of lifestyles we pursue and what is the environmental impact of those lifestyles. It is curious that we have spent several decades being concerned about the growing numbers of humankind while not giving at least an equal amount of attention to the levels of living we aspire to, and how many natural resources we chew up thereby and how much pollution and waste we cause.

Everybody is a consumer of sorts. True, every fifth person scarcely qualifies for that designation, consuming goods worth less than $1 per day. Conversely, every seventh person qualifies for a designation of super-consumer, with a cash income at least fifty times greater. These latter are the people who, through their carbon dioxide emissions, are disrupting everybody's climate dozens of times more than the average citizen of One Earth. Fair play, anyone?

Much as the have-nots seek to match the have's, it is plain their efforts will not work out for a long time to come, at best. If every Chinese person were to consume just one additional chicken per year and if the said chicken were to be raised primarily on grain, this would account for as much grain per year as all the grain exports of the number two exporter, Canada. If the Chinese were to raise their per capita consumption of beef, now only 4 kgs per year, to that of Americans, 45 kg, and if the additional beef were produced largely in feedlots after the manner of the United

States, it would account for as much extra grain as the entire US grain harvest, less than one-third of which is exported. Because of its recent climbing up the food chain toward a meat-based diet, China has become one of the world's leading importers of grain. The global grain market today is around 200 million tons per year, and shows scant scope for significant increase.

As a further measure of its ambitions, the Chinese government has designated the auto industry as one of five industry "pillars". Today China has fewer cars than Los Angeles. If per capita car ownership, together with oil consumption, were to match that of the United States, China would need 80 million barrels of oil per day—by contrast with the world's 1996 oil output of 64 million barrels of oil per day. The surge in carbon dioxide emissions would be unprecedented.

All this notwithstanding, there are already some 250 million newly affluent people in China. They are people with a household income equivalent to perhaps US$20,000, and enough discretionary income to enjoy the perquisites of the good life as perceived by these nouveaux riches. Top of the shopping lists are meat and more meat, followed by cars whether big or small. These are the badges of success: they show you have arrived.

The new consumers in China are matched by at least 200 million in India, and tens of millions in South Korea, Taiwan, Malaysia and Thailand (the recent economic setbacks have not permanently punctured the economic bubbles). Then there are 200 million more in Brazil, Argentina, Venezuela and Mexico, and more again in Hungary and other countries of Eastern Europe, also Turkey. Put them all together and they total about as many as the 800 million long established consumers in the ultra rich countries (the OECD grouping). When the current economic hiccups in Asia are left behind, the ranks of the new consumers can be expected to rise rapidly.

But they cannot hope to become super consumers. Where would all the extra gain come from? How could the global climate tolerate the huge additional pulse of carbon dioxide? There are all kinds of other environmental reasons to suppose that environmental constraints will become all the more constraining. True, technology could help moderate the environmental impact. We could enjoy twice as much material prosperity while using only half as much natural resources and causing half as much pollution and waste. But the new consumers will want to pursue the American dream to the hilt, and it is hard to see that the best technologies could enable huge numbers of affluent aspirants, perhaps two billion people by 2010, enjoying even half the material prosperity of Americans with average household incomes of $40,000.

But is it true "prosperity"—mental and emotional as well as material? Or is the American dream becoming a nightmare with its harried lifestyles and declining leisure time, where the shopping mall is the ultimate mecca, and the good life is a case of piling up goodies?

In any case, we cannot expect the new consumers to forego their "rightful share" of affluence unless the long-time affluent agree to cut back on their environmental ruinous lifestyles. It is these communities that must offer a strong example, and soonest. Where is the political leader who will espouse the new vision, however much it may be perceived as the ultimate vote loser?

28

The Future of Work

The advent of an 'intangible' economy does not mean the end of work. But it does mean the end of familiar routines and rhythms, of job security, of rigid hierarchies and career planning.

People are worried about the far-reaching transformation of the economy. Are we heading for "the end of work". Yes, we have reached the end of the road. We are no longer creating jobs in industry and automation is sure to reduce their number in the services sector. The quantity of work is thus inexorably bound to decrease.

This thesis may be popular, but it is also mistaken and harmful. History shows that technological innovation has always created jobs on a large scale. In no way is the current trend leading to "the end of work". Just the opposite; the new economy contains huge pools of new jobs which can more than make up for the inevitable loss of traditional jobs.

Dematerialisation—the shift away from material products—is revolutionizing all aspects of work—its nature, its organisation and its relationship with other activities. Its function is no longer just the manufacture of physical objects but the handling of data, images and symbols. The content of jobs is becoming more abstract. Skilled workers need to know a lot more about mathematics than their fathers or grandfathers did. Even milking cows and manufacturing require more and more calculation, evaluation and control.

Financial Markets That Never Sleep

The organisation as well as the product of work is also becoming increasingly intangible. The unity of time, space and action which characterized work in the industrial economy has disintegrated. Work is no longer a regular eight-hours-a-day, five-days-a-week routine. New rhythms have appeard—the hectic pace of financial markets which never sleep, the ups-and-downs of life in show business and the uncertainties of "just-in-time" production where components are delivered a few moments before the final product is assembled.

The new jobs are quitting familiar workplaces such as factories, offices and warehouses. Telework is increasing. Europe's teleworkers may number 10 million by the year 2000, up from one million in 1994.

This upheaval of worktime and workspace is going hand in hand with a functional explosion. The range of skills and types of work is expanding all the time. In the United States, the number of job categories has risen from eighty in the 1940s to nearly 800 today. At the same time, trades are dying out faster and faster, especially in information technology where many jobs have a short life of only a few years. Jobs are becoming simultaneously more evanescent and more pervasive, more dissociated and more integrated. On the one hand, fragmentation in time and space seems to be more extensive than it was in the industrial economy. On the other, information technology is strengthening the links between different stages of work and creating an overall fluidity.

Disparities in Productivity

The new forms of work are non-linear. When handling information, knowledge and feelings, there is no direct relationship between the amount of efforts and the final result. This makes of very wide disparities in productivity. In industry, the ratio of the performance of an average worker to that of a good one is no more than one to five. But in immaterial work, an excellent programmer can be a hundred times more productive than an average one.

Non-linear work means non-linear organisation. The notion of a rigid, formal hierarchy based on unchanging criteria no longer makes much sense. All that matters now is technical, scientific or artistic skill and the ability to establish a solid relationship with the customer. Functional hierarchy is replaced by "brainpower"—authority gravitates to those who create and control the new stock of intangible assets: data, brand image, technological know-how and human capital.

The new techniques for managing human resources are individualizing the assessment of performance. Two people doing the same job may have different salaries and different status. Automatic across-the-board pay rises are being dropped and replaced by bonuses linked to results. There are no sinecures in the new business enterprise, either for rank-and-file employees, supervisors or technicians—the supposed beneficiaries of the new knowledge economy.

Business leaders are no longer a protected species. The head of a big American firm is ten times more likely to be sacked for poor performance now than was the case twenty years ago. The notions of loyalty and of indissoluble links between a firm and its employees are losing their meaning.

The changing nature of work has led to a big increase in so-called non-typical jobs, including part-time, temporary and flexi-time work and short-term contracts. Almost all the jobs created in Europe between 1992 and 1996 were part-time. This trend worries many observers who see it as hidden under-employment or disguised unemployment. But they are overly pessimistic. The growth of non-typical jobs is the result of the convergence of several persistent developments.

Where the New Jobs Are?

The shrinking number of jobs in traditional sectors of the economy seems to be a general and irreversible trend. In rich countries as a whole, the share of industrial jobs fell from 28 per cent in 1970 to 18 per cent in 1994. Meanwhile, the share of the services sector grew steadily. Four major new sources of jobs can be identified:

Handling Information and Knowledge: Computer services, research and development, teaching and training account for 40 per cent of knowledge workers. These high-intensity knowledge activities comprised 43 per cent of all new jobs created in the United States between 1990 and 1995, but only 28 per cent of total jobs.

Information Technology: Here there is a shortage of personnel. Professional groups are sounding the alarm and calling on governments to help. In the European Union countries, the imbalance between supply and demand is such that half a million jobs are waiting to be filled.

The Health Sector: The growth of high-intensity knowledge services in this field is related to increased life expectancy and the ageing of the population, and the demand for physical and psychological well-being is also steadily increasing. The growth of expenditure on health is persistent and widespread. For the OECD countries as a whole, this spending grew from 3.9 per cent of GDP in 1960 to 7.2 per cent in 1980 and 8.4 per cent in 1992.

The Leisure Economy: This has triggered the expansion of cultural, sporting and leisure services. It ranges from amusement parks and rock concerts to cultural events such as opera and major art exhibitions. The products of the culture industries have become mass consumer items. Never before have people read so much, listened to so much classical music or visited so many museums. Information technology is also going to add to this vast range of consumer choice. In southern California and New York, the entertainment and multimedia professions are among the main sources of new jobs.

In the labour market, the increase in non-typical jobs is one of the ways in which employers are responding to the pressures of competition and adapting to a global economy which functions seven days a week, twenty-four hours a day. To cope with the new situation, firms are having to figure out how they can use their workers more efficiently and flexibly.

The growth of non-traditional jobs is also due to changing demand. Consumers want to be able to buy a very wide range of goods and services at the drop of a hat, or amuse themselves any time, anywhere. To meet this demand, shops and places of entertainment have to be open late at night and on Sundays. Technology encourages this trend: the virtual economy of the Internet never sleeps.

The widening range of types of work also reflects long-term demographic trends, especially the greater number of women workers and longer life expectancy. Some see non-typical jobs as a necessary evil, while others, especially women with children, welcome the change.

The divide between traditional kinds of work and the new jobs is no longer watertight. People are increasingly switching back and forth between the two categories. In the course of a lifetime, a person may change from full-time to part-time work, from an office job to home office and from the security of a big firm to the adventure of entrepreneurship.

Changes in the nature of work are also breaking down the rigid frontiers, which marked off the world of work. The traditionally distinct fields of work, education and leisure are now interwoven and coexist flexibly in a kind of triple helix of social life.

The emerging intangible and relational economy has a huge potential for growth because it is not bound by the constraints of material scarcity. However, the transition to the new economy is an open-ended process. The state has a key part to play in bringing it about. Governments can slow down the rate of change by making it more painful and more costly.

Obstacles to Change

Pessimistic scenarios are still plausible, such as that of an economy which generates few new jobs and is polarized between a small elite and the rest of the population who are marginalized and lie in precarious conditions. There is a big risk that this scenario will come to pass because current laws and regulations, as well as widespread pessimistic ideas about work, are powerful obstacles to change. Optimistic scenarios require a wholesale reform of institutional structures and profound changes in behavior and attitudes. Such far-reaching changes often run into strong opposition from the social and political establishment and come up against the weight of psychological and social tradition. But the gamble of a new approach to work must be made if the transformation to the intangible economy is to succeed.

29

State Trading Enterprises

Existence of Monopolies is No Longer Justified

Agricultural State Trading Enterprises (STEs), used by some countries to control imports and encourage exports for non-commercial reasons, no longer have a place in global agriculture, STEs not only diminish benefits that other exporters expect in third-country markets, but they may create additional costs for producers, prompt predatory pricing practices that drive other exporters out of particular markets, and keep more producers in business and more land in production than would otherwise be the case.

The new disciplines on agricultural trade established in the Uruguay Round and the globalization of International agricultural trade raise Important questions about the role of state trading enterprises. Traditional reasons for maintaining STEs have included controlling imports, encouraging exports for non-commercial reasons (such as obtaining foreign exchange or removing surplus production), or establishing emergency food stockpiles.

However, rules prohibiting the maintenance of non-tariff barriers through STEs and disciplines on export subsidies have eliminated most of their traditional purposes. As a consequence, agricultural STEs are a concern among many World Trade Organization (WTO) members because of their potential to distort trade. Much of the concern arises from the substantial market power wielded by monopoly STE exporters and importers, commonly referred to as single-desk sellers and buyers. Some of the common characteristics of single-desk sellers and buyers are described here, along with some of the potential trade distortions that may result from the operation of the single-desk system

Single-Desk Sellers

Single-desk sellers have common characteristics that may give them advantages in international trade and may lead to trade distortions. These Include a lack of price transparency; government financial backing that may insulate them from the financial risks normally faced by other exporters; an ability to control procurement costs by maintaining monopsony control over purchases for domestic and export sales; an ability to "price discriminate" using cross-subsidization, either between the domestic and export markets or between different buyers; and the ability to insulate producers from market prices through price-pooling schemes. These characteristics and the distortions that they cause may diminish benefits that other exporters expect in third-country markets. Besides their potential to distort trade, single-desk sellers may create additional costs for produces or allocate inefficiencies caused by production driven by non-market price signals.

Monopoly authority and the lack of transparency in export pricing may provide single-desk sellers with greater pricing flexibility relative to private traders. In the private export trade, commodity prices, which are in effect "replacement values" for exported products, are quoted daily on various market exchanges. Private exporters have no choice but to buy their export supplies at a given market price, which is widely known in the trade and to governments. Single-desk sellers, in contrast, are not required to reveal their transaction prices. This may put them in a position to disguise procurement costs and subsequent export prices, particularly when export sales are subsidized through direct or indirect government subsidies.

Many single-desk sellers benefit from the financial backing of the central government, either through direct subsidies or from government guarantees. Because single-desk sellers are quasi-governmental entities or direct government agencies, their operational losses, which generally have been caused by pooling account deficits, are in most cases reimbursed by the federal government. The actual intervention by the government, or the functional equivalent afforded through the assurance of government intervention, shields producers from risk and encourages production because producers can rely on support when faced with reduced revenue from declining prices. This encourages higher levels of production than otherwise would occur.

Single-desk sellers are monopsony buyers for export and frequently monopolists for re-sales in the domestic market. As such, they can force producers to accept lower prices than might otherwise be possible under more competitive conditions. This is particularly important when a country exports a substantial share of total production. Producers, who frequently have no alternative crops to cultivate for geographic reasons, have no alternative but to sell to the single-desk exporter and take whatever price is offered, giving the single-desk seller wide flexibility in export pricing. Additionally, this control leaves open the opportunity for the single desk seller to reduce, delay, or otherwise manipulate the price it pays producers to acquire supplies. This pricing power may be behind a host of many other practices that can lead to trade distortions, including price discrimination.

In world markets, where prices are normally outside the control of sellers in a particular country, the ability to price discriminate may represent a significant advantage for a single-desk seller. It may also lead to higher levels of imports into particular WTO member countries than would occur under perfectly competitive conditions. Price discrimination occurs when a single-desk seller can differentiate its sales prices for comparable quality commodities between different destinations according to a buyer's ability to pay. The ability to discriminate allows a single-desk seller to maximize returns among a range of purchasers with different price elasticities by lowering prices to certain buyers without affecting its higher sales price in premium markets. Since single-desk sellers control their procurement costs, they have more power to raise and lower prices across different markets. If single-desk sellers are obliged to purchase all domestic production, the ability to price discriminate allows them to lower costs to whatever level is necessary to unload the product in foreign markets. Similarly, when single-desk sellers are driven by government policy objectives, such as maximizing production or exports rather than profits, sales in high-price markets can underwrite the sale of surplus products at uneconomical prices. Additionally, price discrimination encourages the use of predatory pricing practices, whereby a monopoly seller lowers its prices to drive other exporters out of a particular market. If successful, the single-desk seller can raise prices once the competition has been eliminated.

Price-pooling arrangements that are operated by single-desk sellers are intended to equalize payments to producers while minimizing the risk inherent in marketing their products. Under a pooling system, farmers deliver their product to a pool controlled by the single-desk seller in return for an initial payment. At the end of a marketing year, the single-desk seller tallies its total sales revenues and deducts marketing and other operational costs. The net revenue is then distributed to the producers. Under this system, each farmer, in effect, receives a blended price based on all sales for the year.

Diversifying sales reduces the risk borne by producers, but it also leaves all export-pricing decisions to the single-desk seller, which may set prices based on a range of government policy objectives. Although pooling helps reduce market risk for producers by acting to stabilize prices received during the marketing year, costs are inherent in the pooling system. For example, producers of higher-quality products, those that have achieved marketing efficiencies, or those that deliver products to the pool during a period of higher world prices are effectively penalized because they may receive a blended price derived from a lower-quality grade or from revenue generated by lower-priced sales. As a consequence, wealth is transferred from high-quality producers to lower-quality producers, which may keep more producers in business and more land in production than otherwise would be the case.

Single-Desk Buyers

Single-desk buyers may be able to restrict or otherwise distort trade in several ways—lack of transparency, interference with end-users, enforcement of burdensome requirements on imported products, and procurement of emergency stockpiles. These and other purchasing and marketing practices may raise domestic prices and impair market access opportunities for exporters. Monopoly control over imports and the resulting market power of single-desk buyers may allow them to restrict access for imported products based on government-determined criteria, not on commercial considerations. This decision can be made without regard to prevailing world market conditions or domestic demand considerations. Ultimately, this control gives the single-desk buyer the flexibility to support internal prices and to otherwise regulate demand for imports.

Single-desk buyers generally provide insufficient transparency regarding their purchases and sales. Information on import pricing, resale pricing, requested grades and quality, and purchase quantities are not available to traders or the public. Lack of this information makes it difficult for exporters and domestic end-users to do business and may allow the single-desk buyer to disguise trade restrictions.

State control of marketing and distribution may interfere with end-user purchasing decisions—in contrast to direct contact between exporters and end-users, which allows the specification of grade and quality and leads to increased value of imported products to the end-user. This benefits end-users and consumers, but it can also benefit exporters who develop marketing relationships and receive higher prices by dealing with end-users who value the grade and quality of their products. However, when these decisions must go through single-desk importers, the importer can enforce other government policy objectives, such as discouraging imports of competitive grades and qualities or "luxury" that restrict imports.

Single desk buyers may be empowered to enforce burdensome requirements on imported products. Marketing control including control of internal marketing and distribution of imports, also gives the single-desk seller the ability to direct imports of inferior quality products that may be less competitive than domestically produced products. Retail pricing, promotion, and distribution of imported products are often controlled by the single-desk buyer. This may interfere with consumer preferences and efficient resource allocation, especially when marketing strategy is formulated by a state-controlled entity rather than a private firm that is subject to market competition.

❑❑❑

30

The Environment, the Economy and Public Health

An Integrated View

The environment is central to the health of people and their economies. Just as a foetus is totally dependent on the life-support system of the mother during her pregnancy, so the health and vitality of people and their economies are totally dependent on their environments. Unfortunately, many people do not see it that way. They either see the environment as dependent on the economy—such as the politician who says: "let's make the economy strong, then we'll fix the environment when we can afford it"—or they see little connection between health and the environment, whether they are "deep greens" campaigning on ecological issues or doctors treating individual patients and individual illnesses. Whether we are politicians, greens or doctors, is there not a more efficient way to fulfil our aims? For this, a broader perspective is essential.

All economies are sub-systems of the larger environmental system which provides the:

- sources of energy and materials;
- sinks for pollution and other wastes;
- services of water, nutrients and carbon recycling;
- space for living, working and aesthetics ("a walk in the woods and the song of a bird").

Neglect of this life-support system of the "4 S's" leads to weaker or defunct economies as vegetation, food, soils, water or air become contaminated or exhausted and gradually fail to support economic activity. This is dramatically illustrated in the Aral Sea region, or the collapsed Canadian salmon fishing communities.

Indirect Social Costs

Less catastrophic but still costly is where economic damage is caused by pesticides and nutrient contamination of groundwater, involving millions of Rupees in water treatment. This is a social cost to the economy that the agricultural sector does not include in the price of its food: an economic distortion that reduces the real wealth of society via false price signals that encourage the over-use of pesticides and fertilisers. Similarly, the "external" costs on society of road-respiratory-induced accidents, noise, respiratory and circulatory diseases and congestion amount to a lot of money to any government but these costs are not borne by transport users, which mean that transport is encouraged beyond the level that is economic for society as a whole. By internalising these externalities via taxes and other means, the market prices for transport would become fairer and more efficient. Currently only about 30 per cent of transport externalities are covered by transport taxes. But if the health of an economy is dependent on the health of its environment, what about the health of its people?

Without access to the basics of clean water, shelter, fresh air and food, people obviously suffer. Even in more developed economies where the link between everyday life and the environment is not so visible, the role of environmental factors in disease and well-being is significant. Most of the major diseases such as heart disease, cancer, respiratory diseases and allergies have an environmental as well as a genetic component within a multi-factorial chain of causation. And while each environmental factor may be small, if the links in the chain of causation are inter-dependent, as they often appear to be then removing even a small link can break the chain.

Environmental Factors

Take asthma in children, for example. These seem to be many causes, from a child's genetic inheritance to its nutritional status, which in turn help determine how it reacts to the many environmental factors, both indoor (such as mites, pets, damp, environmental tobacco smoke, nitrogen oxides) and outdoor (such as pollen and pollution from industry and traffic), that have been implicated in asthma causation. Therefore it is clear that diagnoses of asthma and many other diseases should systematically embrace environmental factors. This will be a significant challenge for doctors whose time is scarce and whose training is not usually appropriate.

This multi-causal chain will vary in its exact make-up from child to child, but for children overall, even if the evironmental factors such as damp housing to traffic fumes may be less important than, say, genetic make-up or nutritional status, the environmental factors may be the ones that can be most cost effectively removed, thus breaking the causal chain. And, as with many environmental issues, there are secondary benefits of action, such as less noise or fewer accidents from traffic reduction, or energy savings from dry houses, which further justify the environmental actions even where exact causations are not well understood.

The environmental causes of disease and ill-health are a controversial and ill-understood area of science and opinions vary about their significance. Some say that, for Western Europe, perhaps 2-3 per cent of public disease and ill-health is determined by known environmental factors but others maintain that it must be far more significant. They point to the sharp increase over the last two or three decades in asthma, allergies, and cancers (particularly of the reproductive organs such as breast and testicles) and related ill-health such as sperm count decline, which cannot be explained by genetic causes. They also observe that the large differences in health between the socio-economic classes cannot be explained without involving significant environmental causation.

It is thought that the ubiquitous presence of low doses of mixtures of chemicals in food, drink, air, consumer products and the general environment are playing some role in public ill-health, even if the evidence for this is far from substantial.

Impact on Public Health

But what about environmental programmes and campaigns being little concerned with health? Well, history so far shows that the environment only gets serious attention when it is seen to be damaging either the economy or public health. Yet because "everything connects" in "socio-enviro" systems, action to stop infectious diseases from water contamination, or to reduce skin cancer from ozone depletion, leads to a better environment for all species. And if upland forests are preserved because they are seen to be cheaper and more effective water regulators (which reduce the risk of lowland flooding) than dams, then upland biodiversity benefits anyway, even if it was last in the queue for political attention.

Although public health may be seen by some as only a small part of "the environment", much environmental progress depends upon the political weight of the health impacts. For example, the cost benefit exercise on the current multi-pollutant/effect programme on acidification, eutrophication and low-level ozone shows that it is the benefits to human health, not eco-system damage, that provide the main economic justification for further reductions in SO_2, No_x and NH_3. Ecologists need the language of public health in order to maximise political support for the environment. So, it is out of our specialist "boxes" of economics, health and ecology, and into a shared systems approach, with integrated programmes that build partnerships for progress.

❑ ❑ ❑

31

Venture Capital for Small and Medium Business

A Proposal for South-South Cooperation

Although great strides have been made in the last decade to help finance business start-ups for micro-enterprises in low-income countries (LICs), using models such as the Grameen Bank in Bangladesh and others, no similar initiative has been taken to help small and medium enterprises (SMEs) in these countries.

Development banks or other development finance institutions (DFIs) in developing countries are not really meant nor organized to serve the particular needs of their counties' SMEs. They are not only unable to draw on a local capital market to finance their operations, but they also lack the range of advisory services required by SMEs to submit bankable loan applications and are themselves ill-equipped to evaluate such applications. Consequently, they concentrate on a few large projects—preferably of the infrastructure type—for which they rely on the technical expertise of the foreign donors financing them or specially hired consultants.

In the absence of a realistic access to DFIs, SMEs have been constrained to seek their loans for new business ventures from commercial banks. The fact that since 1978 the World Bank has been challenging a large portion of its credit lines intended for SMEs through commercial banks rather than through DFIs, reflects the importance which donors attach to the role of LIC commercial banks as the principal intermediaries for SME lending.

Reasons for Failure of Traditional Banking Systems

However, there are several important reasons why commercial banks are ill-suited to perform this task. First and foremost, the banking systems of these countries were conceived during a period when most investment capital was provided by the government, usually drawing on foreign aid. Thus, even in those LICs which had not entirely succumbed to the socialist ideology in the sense of eliminating all private enterprise, commercial banks continue to limit their credit activity largely to self-liquidating, low-risk credits seldom exceeding 12 month's duration, preferably conventional trade credits. Secondly, even in the exceptional cases where commercial banks in these countries entertain applications for medium-term credits to finance the launching of a small manufacturing project, they will normally demand ironclad collateral in the forms of liens on real-estate and/or personal guarantees by friends and relatives with similar backing, unless the applicant is a well-known customer of the bank. Thirdly, with their overriding concern for profitability, most LIC commercial banks tend to like upon business start-up loans to SMEs as being too risky and/or administratively too costly to handle in relation to the loan amounts involved. For these reasons, commercial banks in these countries are unlikely to establish in-house facilities to meet the specific needs of SMEs, such as helping them in project preparation and market analysis. Last but not least, factors such as the project's development orientation" (e.g. its important substitution and export potential, its ability to increase productivity and its employment generation features) do not enter into the calculations of commercial banks which will orient their actions towards "bottom line" results and risk minimization. Under the circumstances, most commercial banks are not inclined to become directly involved in project supervision, as long as their customer's repayment records are satisfactory.

Credit for SMEs

Whereas new approaches have been developed over the last decade by various development assistance agencies to help up-grade commercial banks' staff capability, especially in advising SME borrowers in such matters as project formulation and market analysis as well as improving and market analysis as well as improving their loan repayment capacity, only recently has an effort been made to find ways and means of making investment capital available to SME entrepreneurs for launching new businesses. In some LICs, lines of credit have been established by multilateral or bilateral banks from which loan capital can be sought for such projects, but only; seldom has genuine risk (i.e., equity) capital been made available and when some only; through the donors' own agencies. The interest rate charged by the local a banks for administering loans from these credit lines in local currency are generally; at a par with existing commercial rates, which tend to be prohibitive for a new venture of the type being promoted. These high rates are due to several factors, including (a) the local rates of inflation and the consequent devaluation risks, (b) the high risk factor of the new enterprises with little or no collateral and credit standing, and (c) the lack of experience of bank staff in the evaluation of loan requests submitted to them for unfamiliar projects. Significantly, most international DFIs are loath to lower interest rates to be applied on loans financed by their credit lines, lest they be accused of unfair competition on the local financial markets.

Incentives Ineffective in Attracting Foreign Investors

Although many international conferences, investment promotion meetings and other fora have been staged by UN bodies and donor groups to generate private investor interest in the LICs, these efforts have proved largely ineffectual. While much has been done by LIC governments in recent years to create a more attractive "enabling environment" for private investment, these incentives have been necessary but not sufficient to convince developed-country enterprises or investors to assume the necessary risks, with the exception of selected sectors such as mineral extraction, tourism and a narrow range of exportable consumer goods, such as out-of-season fruits and vegetables, and tropical products such as cocoa and certain spices. Even public support for project preparation has ultimately failed to provide preparation has ultimately failed to provide private business in industrial countries the incentives needed to take an active role in a broadly-based economic development of LICs.

The bottom line for potential investors in LICs is constituted by the profits which their investment will yield within a reasonable period of time, under conditions which offer a reasonable amount of political and legal stability. So far, these basic conditions have not been met on the whole. In the new global economy with its almost total reliance on free market principles and the ability to choose investment sites freely, the choice is not likely to fall on the LICs, but rather on a small number of more advanced developing countries, apart from the industrial countries themselves.

South-to-South Technological/Commercial Cooperation

While the inherent disadvantages faced by LICs in competing for foreign investment capital are too great to be overcome by a magic panacea, any attempt at a solution must include measures designed to mobilize the entrepreneurial abilities and dynamism available in existing and potential SMEs engaged in production of a variety of goods destined for the broad consumer market at home and abroad. In most LICs such existing or potential SMEs need to access affordable foreign technologies, i.e., the machinery and the technological know-how required to install and make the machinery function. One of the prime sources of such technologies for LICs can be found in enterprises in South/Southeast Asia and China, countries that have only recently graduated from the LIC status (or have not yet done so but have nevertheless managed to create a modern industrial sector within their overall state of underdevelopment and poverty). The concretization of transfers of technology from these countries to the LICs is especially affected by the financing problems described above, because in the normal case neither one of the potential partners can afford the necessary venture, even though they can and will invest their know-how, time and very often land, buildings and infrastructure. This problem is much less acute in the case of the more expensive, and hence often unaffordable "Northern" technologies, where the technology provider finds it easier to mobilize start-up capital from its own resources or by; borrowing from his commercial bank against his firms' overall credit line.

The underlying economic rationale in favour of such South-to South, company-tocompany transfers of production technology argues that Asian firms can help launch industrial start-ups in these countries far more cheaply and quickly than the more sophisticated companies from the North. By offering labour-intensive rather than capital intensive production machinery accompanied by vitally needed on the-job training, back-up managerial and maintenance follow-up at a fraction of the cost of Northern firms, Asian companies' cooperation can spell the difference between a successful business start-up and a failed one. Furthermore Asian-sourced machinery can be operated at production scales corresponding to the reduced market requirements and limited purchasing power of most LIC markets.

In view of the above described financing problems faced by South-to-South deals, it is proposed that a Venture Capital Fund be established specializing in the provision of equity capital for joint ventures (JVs) among SMEs in various LICs. In many cases the existence of such a FUND —which might be called the VENTURE CAPITAL FUND or simply (VENCAP)—will spell the difference between business proposals that are still-born for want of the required initial financing, and profitable ventures which are launched thanks to the missing—if minority—equity contribution from the FUND.

Characteristics of the FUND

The proposed VENCAP would be expected to be an active participant in the project in which it will invest, sharing its financial and strategic vision with the invested firm. To this end, it must have access to experienced project evaluation specialists with intimate knowledge of conditions in low-income countries in general, and the project and its promoters in particular. As might be expected, the FUND would concentrate its resources in early-state financing, rather than in plant expansion or replacement, inasmuch as the projects likely to be the most profitable are the new ones, which will normally start from empty factory buildings and offices, where only a minimum amount of production equipment, if any, is normally usable for the operation of the new JV.

The FUND would limit its participation to joint ventures in which firms of at least two developing countries hold equity stakes, although firms from developed countries might also participate. The FUND would limit its participation to production JVs whose total initial capital would not exceed a given sum to be determined. Its own participation would in turn also be limited by a relative ceiling per venture i.e., a maximum percentage of the total capital. This combination would implicitly set an absolute ceiling to the FUND's participation in any given JV.

Success and Selection Criteria

The number of proposed projects must be sufficient to allow the FUND to pick and choose the best. A good ratio of applications to acceptances might be in the range of 10:1 Whereas commercial viability will constitute the first and foremost selection criterion, every effort would be made to select projects which have a strong development character, are environmentally friendly and/or involve production technologies which are deemed to be vital and critical to the recipient country's current socio-economic needs. Thus, preference would be given to sectors such as (a) food processing (b) water purification, (c) renewable energy (d) agricultural development, and (e) light engineering. In all cases, the emphasis would be on cost-effective, labour-intensive production technologies.

The FUND's ability to divest itself of its participation at a profit will be the ultimate test of the FUND's success. Ideally, the FUND should be able to do this within a maximum of one or two years, so as to enable it to effectively cycle its resources to other equally meritorious projects.

Proposals for VENCAP's Organisational Structure

Besides being run by an experienced FUND manager, VENCAP would be assisted in its investment decisions by National Advisory Committees (NACs), which; would be established in all participating LICs and would be composed of prominent business persons, professional men and women and financiers. These NACs would be chaired by an experienced consultant/consulting firm selected by the FUND. No member of the NAC having business or family links with the person or firm applying for equity financing would participate in the evaluation procedure. VENCAP would be represented on the Boards of Directors of the firms in which it has acquired minority stakes through one or several members of the relevant; NAC. The FUND itself would be run by a Board of Directors in which all of the major investors would be represented (and possibly some NGOs, PVOs).

Follow-up

It is hoped that this article will provoke sufficient interest to justify the convening of an international meeting of aid agency officials and experts to study the ideas set forth above, so as to facilitate VENCAP's formal launching as an operative force. The need is there, the customer are there, the goodwill is there, only the financing and the organization are lacking!

❑ ❑ ❑

32

No Progress Without a Secular Society

Every day, women continue to be victims of rape, trafficking, acid-throwing, dowry deaths and other kinds of torture. At the opening of this new century, women are still not considered as equal human beings in many parts of the world. Religion and patriarchy continue to have an all-encroaching hold on their lives, maintaining and justifying their age-old oppression. In some South Asian Societies, this hold is even increasing.

I do not believe that there can be real equality in a society dominated by religion. Western countries speak repeatedly about the necessity of economic development to alleviate poverty. But this is not enough. Some oil rich countries may be economically developed, but women are deprived of all rights. The supremacy of religion is incompatible with freedom of expression, women's rights and democracy. This is why I see religion as the main enemy of women's development.

We have to act on several fronts at once. First of all, improving access to education. In a society like Bangladesh, 80 per cent of women are illiterate. For centuries women have been taught they are the slaves of men. It is very hard to change their minds, to make them aware of their oppression, to give them a sense of their independence. This educational effort has to go hand in hand with a secular feminist movement in society. Such movements have to start within the country and they cannot take hold when people are uneducated and unaware of their oppression. I'm not sure you can accomplish much from the outside, except to expose in the media the atrocities women in all too many countries face in their day to day lives.

In some countries, this movement is emerging, but very timidly, and it has a slim margin of maneuver. It has the uphill task of fighting for the repeal of religious laws and the introduction of a uniform civil code. So far, it tends to be constituted by a few individual feminists who are forced to be diplomatic, to compromise with fundamentalists, be they men or women. But they are trying to change the system, step by step, and it will take a very long time. People are not yet ready to do away with religious laws that impact upon every aspect of society, from education and health to the workplace and the home.

For women's status to change, we also need enlightened leaders who believe in equality. In countries of South Asia women with a strong voice do not have the support of political leaders, whether they be men or women. Look at the countries in which women are in politics, or even heads of state. Does it follow that women in those countries are emancipated? Because of long-standing vested interests, such leaders continue to back measures that oppress women. They are not ideologically committed to changing these conditions. In South Asia, most of the women who become heads of state are religious, and like men, they adhere to the religious objectives of the establishment. Until a society is not based on religion and women and considered equal to men before the law, I do not think that politics will advance the cause of women.

Until a society is not based on religion and women are considered equal to men before the law, I do not think that politics will advance the cause of women. In Western countries, women are educated, they are treated equally, they have access to jobs. In these conditions, their participation in politics has a meaning.

Education, a secular feminist movement and leaders—both men and women—committed to equality and justice. This is what it will take to change the dire conditions which too many women still face today. It will take a very long time, but we are here to work towards that end.

33

Resistance to Change

Why Poverty Reduction Programmes Did Not Work

Poverty reduction as an overall objective of the global development industry is not new. The only problem is that so far it has not really worked. Despite several decades of economic growth and huge development aid disbursements, the number of countries the United Nations calls "least developed" (those with a per capita income of less than US$ 900 a year) has in fact nearly doubled since 1971, from 25 to 49. In the last decade (1990-2000) and despite all development efforts—not even one country was able to graduate from this group to a higher income level, may be with the exception of Botswana.

Meanwhile, poverty reduction has generated its own history. This programme has covered a wide range of approaches starting from the World Banks's small-farmers-strategies in the 1970s via the costly structural adjustment policies of the 1980s to the recent poverty reduction strategies of the 1990s. Once more, the next development decade (2000-2010) has written "Attacking Poverty" on its banner. It seems that something must have gone wrong along the way. What (bitter?) lessons have been learnt from previous experience? Have they been factored into the new set of policies? Were there possibly some fundamental flaws which were overlooked, and can better results be expected during the next period? Or do the many failures and disappointments demonstrate that there is some systemic "resistance to change" by those in power in the least developed countries and perhaps also by the poor themselves?

1. What Can the Rural Poor Really Expect from Poverty Reduction Programmes?

In India, of example, 70 per cent of the people still earn their livelihood in the agricultural sector; most of the poor among them live in a kind of rural subsistence economy. People who live in a subsistence economy are naturally conservative. They are busy securing their survival and are very reluctant to take risks. Their living standard is measured in amounts of rice harvested; their wealth is measured in numbers of livestock. Within this simple framework, poor peasants behave very rationally. For example, a shift from food crops to cash crops, such as from rice to coffee or tapioca, would immediately endanger their subsistence in case of failure. Furthermore, the poor do not have the knowledge and skills to change their crops quickly in response to market demands. Moving from a subsistence economy to a commodity economy is therefore a big step for small farmers.

However, poor people are always happy to receive handouts from the Government like fertiliser, seeds, medicine or blankets. Roads, bridges and schools are also very welcome. Who would refuse a gift? From their point of view, it is the responsibility of the Government to distribute goods and services in the form of aid programmes as a way to share some of the prosperity of the city people with them. Nevertheless, as they see no direct and immediate benefit for themselves, they tend to take a rather passive attitude to change. Development workers have often complained about this common apathy and about the lack of will among the poor themselves to improve their situation. In the final analysis, rural development is more a problem of providing the right economic incentives for change than of overcoming traditional thinking and a conservative attitude.

2. What Kind of Incentives are Necessary to Achieve Increased Production in the Countryside?

In most poor countries the key to rural development is the problem of land ownership rights and of legal security. As long as people do not own the land that they cultivate, they are not interested in making any investments, be they in the form of labour or capital. Once a farmer has an ownership title and considers the land as his own, he will refrain from overusing the soil but shift crops and plant new trees. Moreover, he can then use his land as collateral for credits or even sell it and buy land somewhere else.

In addition to clear and irrevocable ownership rights, the rule of law is another crucial factor for development. People must feel safe from abuse of power by local elites and corrupt government officials. They must be able to enforce their basic rights in an impartial court of law. Furthermore, they must be safe from land expropriation without adequate compensation and from resettlement against their will. In other words, it is primarily their very stake holdership in the rural economy that will motivate them to increase their production. Of course, the other necessary incentives are access to markets, a fair price for their products and the availability of goods and services.

3. Poverty Reduction Programmes, if Not Accompanied by Parallel Institutional Reforms, Run the Risk of Creating a Modern Version of the Cargo Cult

Cargo cults spread during World War II in the highlands of Papua New Guinea at a time when several US cargo planes loaded with food supplies crashed into the hills. Suddenly, the native people could enjoy an abundant amount of goods, which literally fell down on them like a "gift from heaven". In the hope of attracting some more of these "silvery birds", the local hill tribes constructed primitive models of airplanes, sat around them in a circle, and prayed that more "cargo" would drop on their territory. As this happened in some areas (albeit as a result of the air battle between Japan and the USA), it strengthened the belief in the cargo cult as some magical way to overcome poverty, at least for a short time.

There is a high risk that aid programmes under the banner of poverty reduction will create new "cargo cults" in the 49 least developed countries if they continue to carry out their "business as usual" and do not put strong emphasis on the rule of law and civil rights. Unfortunately, the setting up of reliable legal and social institutions in poor countries (which often seems to be the "software" of the development industry accompanying disbursements) is, in fact, as decades of experience have shown, the hard part of the process. But it is also indispensable for achieving any tangible results.

Why have there been until now only modest results in the areas of land reform, rule of law and the guarantee of basic civil rights? Why have people's participation and people's ownership as a strategy hardly taken root at all in the least developed countries? The answer must be sought in the role of powerful local groups and their vested interest, who obviously benefit from the prevailing status quo and a loose legal environment. A cargo cult promises bounty for all recipients; poverty reduction, however, means changing the rural power structure, too.

Conclusion

To insist on the rule of law, on people's participation in the development process, and on transparency and accountability, is again nothing new. Good political and administrative institutions go hand in hand with economic growth. The potential of economic development is quite limited if it works in a framework of social undevelopment and official indifference. Again the question is, who has so little been achieved in this field during previous decades? Was it the wrong medicine and why were the poor results of the aid programmes so carefully ignored by the international donor community?

Looking at the political systems of the 49 least developed countries, it is obvious that most of these countries are "more democratic in principle than in practice". Many of them are ruled by military or civil authoritarian regimes which are more used to giving orders than to listening to the grievances of the poor, Other governments, such as India, are "genuinely democratic at most levels but have historically found it difficult that political accountability reaches all levels of decision-making, particularly for the poor."

To sum up, it seems that resistance to change is equally shared by the cumbersome and often incompetent bureaucracies of the poor countries and the equally cumbersome international donor community, which has so far conveniently kept the call for more rural democracy and people's rights on the backburner. The major reason for the reluctance of the donor community to pursue the battle for the rule of law and the fight against endemic corruption was to avoid massive political confrontation with the receiver countries.

Would it not have been better to create proper incentives for the performance of poor countries, namely by halting loans to nations that do not manage their economies and their reform commitments effectively and increasing financial and technical support to those that do? The next decade will show how determined both local governments and donors are to tackle these problems for the sake of a better future.

34

Stop Child Labour!

Although the internationally recommended minimum age for work is 15 years and the number of child workers under the age of 10 is far from negligible, almost all the data available on child labour concerns the 10 to 14 age group.

Traditionally, the proportion of working children has been much higher in rural than in urban areas—nine out of ten are engaged in agricultural or related activities. In the towns and cities of India where child labour has increased steadily as a result of the rapid urbanisation of recent years, working children are found mainly in trade and services and to a lesser extent in the manufacturing section.

Available statistics suggest that more boys than girls work. It should be borne in mind, however, that the number of working girls is often under estimated by statistical surveys, as they usually do not take into account full-time housework performed by many children, the vast majority of whom are girls, in order to enable their parents to go to work.

Girls, moreover, tend to work longer hours, on average, than do boys. This is especially true for the many girls employed as domestic workers, a type of emloyment in which hours of work are typically extremely long. This is also the case of girls employed in other types of jobs who, in addition to their professional activity, must help with the housework in their parents' home.

One of the factors affecting the supply of child labour is the high cost, in real terms, of obtaining an education. Many children work to cover the costs of school expenses. But, many schools serving the poor are of such abysmal quality or chances of upward mobility for graduates are so slim, that the expected return is not equal to the sacrifice made.... While it is true that many children drop out of school because they have to work. It is equally true that many become so discouraged by school that they prefer to work.

In manufacturing industries, children are most likely to be employed when their labour is less expensive or less troublesome than that of adults, when other labour is scarce, and when they are considered irreplaceable by reason of their size or perceived dexterity.

Many working children face significant threats to their health and safety. The majority are involved in farming and are routinely exposed to harsh climate, sharpened tools, heavy loads as well, increasingly, as to toxic chemicals and motorized equipment. Others, particularly girls working as domestic servants away from their homes, are frequent victims of physical, mental and sexual abuses which can have devastating consequences on their health.

Prostitution is another type of activity in which children, especially girls, are increasingly found. The AIDS epidemic is a contributing factor to this trend, as adults see the use of children for sexual purposes as the best means of preventing infection. The laissez-faire attitude of the authorities incharge of national and international tourism is also largely responsible for the current situation

Another extremely serious problem is child slavery in India. A large number of child slaves are to be found in agriculture, domestic help, the sex industry, the carpet and textile industries, quarrying and brickmaking. Child slavery predominates mainly where there are social systems based on the exploitation of poverty, such as debt bondage, when the motivation is the debt incurred by a family to meet a social or religious obligation or simply to acquire the means of survival.

There is a growing body of opinion that national and international efforts need to be more sharply focused on the most abusive and hazardous forms of child labour, granting them first concern and priority. Perhaps the most telling social argument against child labour is that its effects are highly discriminatory, adding to the burden and disadvantage of individuals and groups already among the socially excluded while benefiting those who are privileged. For that reason, child labour is inconsistent with democracy and social justice.

Action Required at the National Level

In the majority of states of India where child labour is common, the action taken until now to combat it has in no way been proportional to the extent and gravity of the problem. Many state governments have left it to economic growth and legislation alone to provide the solution. Experience has shown however that, unless specific measures are taken, growth in itself rarely benefits the very poor and that legislation means little where it is not vigorously enforced.

The problem of child labour will not be solved overnight. It is one of the many facets of poverty and underdevelopment. Resources available to reduce its extent and damaging effects are by definition scarcest in India that need them the most. Priorities must therefore be set.

No Effective Programmes Without Hard Information

Research: Almost everywhere, hard information is lacking on how many children are working, what they are doing, where and in which conditions. Without such data, it is virtually impossible to develop effective policies and programmes. Establishing, in some cases improving, data collection systems on child labour is an essential first step.

Raising awareness: A common attitude toward child labour in India is to accept it as an unavoidable consequence of poverty. Given the low quality and implied costs of the education services available to the poor, many parent, having themselves worked as children, tend to consider an early entry into the labour market, rather than schooling, as the best way to equip their children with skills useful for their future as adults.

Another difficulty is inherent in the fact that children working in rural areas, in urban informal sector workshops or as domestic servants in private households are not readily visible. An effective effort to protect children from workplace hazards or abuses must therefore begin by making the invisible visible. Experience clearly shows that significant public pressure is required to make progress on the child labour issue politically possible. As long as the general public, and in particular the middle and higher classes, consider that child labour is part of the harsh reality that makes good economic sense, the conditions for change will not be met.

The Government of India has restricted its role to enacting legislation, but has been passive in its enforcement. Most initiatives against child labour have traditionally come from Non-Government Organisations. In spite of their dedication however, their resources cannot be equal to the magnitude of the task. All levels of society need to do their share.

Some types of action can be provided only by the Central Government: child labour legislation and attendant enforcement mechanisms, the setting of public policy priorities and a publicly-funded system of basic education that offers quality schooling for all, including the children of the poorest families.

Trade Unions Bring Abuses to Light

Trade unions, are the logical leaders for bringing child labour abuses to light. They are ideally placed to document concrete cases of abusive child labour and to monitor the effectiveness of legal instruments and the performance of the labour inspectorate in the child labour field.

Employers and their organisations also have good reasons to be interested in the issue. Besides obvious humanitarian and social reasons, combating child labour makes perfect sense on economic and business grounds. Emotionally or physically damaged children have little chance of becoming productive adults.

NGOs' Strength is with Children Already Working

Like trade unions, NGOs can help to discover and publicize specific cases of abusive child labour. They are, in addition especially good at devising and implementing action programmes on behalf of children already in the labour market. Close to the children, they generally enjoy the trust of the local communities concerned and are well placed to appeal to their hearts and resources.

The participation of other segments of civil society—the media, universities, parliamentarians, teachers and educators—should be enlisted in the fight against child labour. All are valuable allies and can cooperate in complementary ways.

Establishing the required institutional capacity: To formulate and execute a national plan of action against child labour, institutional mechanisms must be established or strengthened within the governmental apparatus. These can then be entrusted with the responsibility for setting priorities, coordinating the activities of the various ministries concerned, promoting private sector participation and for launching and supporting pilot schemes to find new way of preventing child labour and of rehabilitating those who have been rescued from it.

Improving legislation and enforcement measures: In India legislation exempts from coverage precisely the kinds of work in which children are most engaged (agriculture, family undertakings, small workshops, domestic service). A necessary first step to expanding protection under the law is to ensure that the main places where children work and the worst forms of child labour are encompassed by national legislation.

Improving schooling for the poor: The single most effective way to stem the flow of school-age children into abusive forms of employment or work is to extend and improve schooling so that it will attract and retain them. Recent trends however leave little room for optimism in that regard. In the eighties and early nineties resources devoted to education have dwindled steadily in India. The poor situation of the economy and the effects of structural adjustment policies were the reasons generally given for this decline.

Using economic incentives: As poor families need the income deriving from the employment of their children, it has often been considered appropriate to provide cash or in-kind payments as replacement.

Lively international debate over negative incentives: The advisability of using negative economic incentives has been the subject of much recent public debate. In Europe several department stores have decided not to sell products such as carpets unless they are certified to be made without child labour. Such movements by consumers and manufacturers alike have been accompanied by powerful efforts on the legislative and trade fronts as demonstrated by the hot debate on the incorporation of a social clause into international trade agreements. The United States has introduced conditionality into its Generalized System of Preferences, as has the European Union, to promote, among others, better labour standards and thereby discourage the use of child labour. A bill aiming at banning the import, into the United States, of goods produced by children (the Harkin Bill), has generated concern among employers and governments in countries heavily dependent on the United States for their exports.

There is no doubt that initiatives of this kind have helped significantly to raise public awareness about child labour. However, they have also had unintended consequences. The mere threat led employers of various industries to abruptly dismiss tens of thousands of children.

35

Energy and Sustainability

Mankind's history is marked by a growing use of energy which until the end of the Industrial Revolution came largely from renewable sources. It was coal that fed the furnaces and boilers of the Industrial Revolution from the end of the seventeenth century to the nineteenth century, and drove railway transport and steamships. As well as being a useful source of mechanical energy, it was also used in the manufacture of coal gas for street lighting and in the chemical industry. In fact, coal was the principal form of energy until 1900.

Discoveries at the beginning of the nineteenth century allowed the use of electricity and revealed the relations and the interconvertibility of different forms of energy. The principles of conservation and of energy quality did not become operative until much later. Meanwhile, in 1882, the first system for producing and distributing electricity in a large city was installed. This was the beginning of the second phase in industrialisation through electrification.

Following the first successful oil drillings in 1859, Standard Oil, the first of the modern large scale oil companies, attempted the first vertical structure for overall control of the oil process. It involved extraction from the subsoil, storage, refining and final distribution. Later, the growth of derivatives, the lower extraction costs compared to coal and the greater ease and economy of transport made oil modern society's basic energy source.

The internal combustion engine led to motorisation on a massive scale by land, sea and air and guaranteed a constantly growing market for petrol. The forties marked the start of the new petrochemical industry, which gave rise to an enormous number of new products; synthetic rubber, plastic, medicines, cosmetics, varnishes, artificial fibres, detergents, weedkillers, fertilizers, butane, propane, etc., opening the way to the mass-production of consumer goods and introducing new, non-biodegradable substances into the environment.

After World War II, ambitious programmes to produce electricity from nuclear energy were begun, in the search for a return on the enormous amounts of money invested. The economic expansion in the West during the fifties and sixties was directly related to enormous petrol consumption at a time when energy was considered plentiful and cheap. Energy consumption during these decades grew more than exponentially. The fastest developing industrial sectors were precisely the ones that consumed most energy—petrochemical industries, metallurgy, car manufacturing, domestic appliances, electricity generating, etc.—and a trend developed towards goods and services with higher energy intensity. Since 1950, increased energy production has been systematically favoured over more rational use. So much so that the increase in energy consumption has been taken as a reliable indicator of progress.

The Aftermath of the Oil Boom

The oil crises of 1973 and 1980 showed up the fragility of an energy system that was over-dependent on oil. The War in the Gulf was reminder of what was at stake for the Western economies; free access to cheap oil in the Middle East. It was therefore fear of the hardship caused by the first crisis that brought about a change in attitudes in Western countries; efforts were directed at breaking free from this dependence, diversifying supply sources, perfecting replacement energies and promoting energy-saving programmes.

The eighties marked a change in people's awareness about environmental problems. The damage was making itself felt in more and more places and eventually the global threat to our planet as a result of our energy system became clear; the composition of the atmosphere was changing and could lead to possible changes in the climate.

According to recent figures, 82 per cent of all the energy consumed in the world is produced by burning fossil fuels, 7.5 per cent from burning biomass, 5.5 per cent from the use of hydraulic energy and 5 per cent from nuclear energy. Most of our energy in other words, in non-renewable; it runs out as we use it, as the population increases; and it comes from fossil fuels, which on burning increase the amount of CO_2 in the atmosphere. If we add to this the accumulation of nuclear waste, the problems of access to oil deposits, constant spillages during transport and all the different imbalances involved in the world energy system, the outlook is far from sustainable.

The inequalities speak for themselves, globally, less than a quarter of the world's richest population consumes almost three quarters of the energy commercialized in the world. For example, the average annual consumption per capita in the United States is 26 times higher than in India.

The Choice of Change

Opening the way to societies that make sustainable use of energy necessarily involves increasing and improving energy efficiency, both in supply technologies and in end-use technologies, at the same time using renewable energy sources instead of fossil fuels.

Choosing the right system for the transformation of primary energy sources into energy services such as lighting, cooling, cooking, mechanical force, transport, etc. and choosing the most suitable appliances and technologies in each case is fundamental.

The truth is that a good standard of living is possible without wasting anything like as much energy. A series of relatively straightforward measures today allow a far higher level of comfort than in 1950, using one-third as much energy for heating water for washing in the home.

Petrol consumption by vehicles has dropped by 40 per cent in forty years, from 8 litres/100 kilometres to 5.3 litres in some models, and the work of improving their energy efficiency continues. In industry, the energy consumption necessary for manufacturing large intermediary products (steel, cement, paper or fertilizer) is decreasing steadily at a rate which varies between 0.5 per cent and 0.2 per cent per year according to the product.

Today's incandescent bulbs consume one twentieth as much electricity as bulbs in the twenties. The compact fluorescent bulbs now available can cut this down again to one-fifth. Efficiency in lighting has increased one-hundredfold. The use of new materials and a more rational use of traditional materials allows a reduction in the amount of energy and raw materials consumed. Building a house, for example, requires 20 per cent less energy than in 1950; building a vehicle, 40 per cent less. On a global level, reducing our society's energy-intensiveness is the first step towards energy sustainability.

❑ ❑ ❑

Bibliography

Agarwal, Bina. 1992. "Gender Relations and Food Security: Coping with Seasonality, Drought and Famine in South Asia." In Lourdes Benería and Shelley Feldman (eds.), *Unequal Burden: Economic Crises, Persistent Poverty, and Women's Work*. Boulder, Colo.: Westview Press.

Agarwal, Bina. 1997. "Bargaining and Gender Relations: Within and Beyond the Household." *Feminist Economics* 3(1): 1-51.

Akerlof, George A., and Rachel E. Kranton. 1999. *Economics and Identity*. Washington, D.C.: Brookings Institute.

Alkire, Sabina. 1999. "Operationalizing Amartya Sen's Capability Approach to Human Development: A Framework for Identifying 'Valuable' Capabilities," Ph.D. diss., Oxford University.

Baulch, Bob., 1996a. "Neglected Trade-Offs in Poverty Measurement." *IDS Bulletin* 27(1): 36-42.

Baulch, Bob., 1996b. "The New Poverty Agenda: A Disputed Consensus." *IDS Bulletin* 27(1): 1-10.

Bebbington A., and T. Perreault. 1999. "Social Capital, Development and Access to Resources in Highland Ecuador." *Economic Geography*. October.

Benería, Lourdes. 1989. "Gender and the Global Economy." In Arthur MacEwan and William Tabb, eds., *Instability and Change in the Global Economy*. New York: Monthly Review Press.

Berelson, Bernard. 1954. "Content Analysis." *Handbook of Social Psychology*. Vol. 1. Reading, Mass.: Addison-Wesley.

Bhatt, Mihir. 1999. "Natural Disasters as National Shocks to the Poor and Development." Disaster Mitigation Institute, Ahmedabad, India.

Booth, David, Jeremy Holland, Jesko Hentschel, Peter Lanjouw, and Alicia Herbert. 1998. *Participation and Combined Methods in African Poverty Assessment: Renewing the Agenda.* Department for International Development (DFID), U.K.: Social Development Division and Africa Division.

Bradley, Christine. 1994. "Why Male Violence Against Women is a Development Issue: Reflections from Papua New Guinea." In Miranda Davies, ed., *Women and Violence: Realities and Responses, Worldwide.* London: Zed Books.

Brunetti, Aymo, Gregory Kisunko, and Beatrice Weder. 1997. "Institutions in Transition: Reliability of Rules and Economic Performance in Former Socialist Countries." Policy Research Working Paper 1809. Washington, D.C.: World Bank.

Carvalho, Soniya, and Howard White. 1997. "Combining the Quantitative and Qualitative Approaches to Poverty Measurement and Analysis: The Practice and the Potential." Technical Paper 366. Washington, D.C.: World Bank.

Castellas, Manuel. 1997. *The Power of Identity.* Malden, Mass.: Blackwell Publishers.

Cernea, Michael. 1979. "Entry Points for Sociological Knowledge in the Project Cycle." Agricultural and Rural Development Department. Washington, D.C.: World Bank.

Cernea, Michael. ed., 1985. *Putting People First.* New York: Oxford University Press.

Cernea, Michael With the Assistance of April Adams. 1994. "Sociology, Anthropology and Development: An Annotated Bibliography of World Bank Publications 1975-1993." Environmentally and Sustainable Development Studies and Monograph Series 3. Washington, D.C.: World Bank.

Cernea, Michael, and Ayse Kudat. 1997. "Social Assessments for Better Development: Case Studies in Russia and

Central Asia." Environmentally Sustainable Development Studies and Monograph Series 16. Washington, D.C.: World Bank.

Chambers, Robert. 1989. "Editorial Introduction: Vulnerability, Coping and Policy." *IDS Bulletin* 20: 1.

Chambers, Robert. 1994. "The Origins and Practice of Participatory Rural Appraisal." *World Development* 22(7). Washington, D.C.: World Bank.

Chambers, Robert. 1997. "Whose Reality Counts? Putting the First Last." London: Intermediate Technology Publications.

Chambliss, William J. 1999. *Power, Politics, and Crime.* Boulder, Colo.: Westview Press.

Charmes, Jacques. 1998. "Informal Sector, Poverty and Gender: A Review of Empirical Evidence." Contributed Paper for *World Development Report 2000.* Washington, D.C.: World Bank, October.

Dahle, Cheryl. 1999. "Social Justice—Alan Khazei and Vanessa Kirsch." Fast Company, Issue 30, December 1999, www. fastcompany.com.

Dasgupta, Partha, and Ismail Serageldin. 1999. *Social Capital: A Multifaceted Perspective.* Washington, D.C.: World Bank.

Davies, Miranda. ed., 1994. *Women and Violence: Realities and Responses Worldwide.* London: Zed Books.

Dollar, David, and Roberta Gatti. 1995. "Gender Inequality, Income, and Growth: Are Good Times Good for Women?" Policy Research Report on Gender and Development, No. 1. Wahington, D.C.: World Bank.

Economist Intelligence Unit. 1997. *Armenia Country Profile, 1996-97.* London: The Economist Intelligence Unit, Ltd.

Edwards, Michael, and David Hulme, eds., 1992. *Making a Difference: NGOs and Development in a Changing World.* London: Earthscan Publications.

Edwards, Robert, and Michael W. Foley. 1997. "Social Capital and the Political Economy of Our Discontent." *American Behavioural Scientist,* 40(5): 669-78.

Esman, Milton J., and Norman Uphoff. 1984. *Local Organisations: Intermediaries in Rural Development.* Ithaca, N.Y.: Cornell University Press.

Fajnzylber, Pablo, David Lederman, and Norman Loayza. 1998. *What Causes Violent Crime?* Office of the Chief Economist, Latin America and the Caribbean Region. Washington, D.C.: World Bank.

Floro, Maria Sagrario. 1995. "Economic Restructuring, Gender and the Allocation of Time." *World Development* 23: 1913-29. Washington, D.C.: World Bank.

Folbre, Nancy. 1991. "Women on Their Own: Global Patterns of Female Headship." In Rita S. Gallin, Anne Ferguson, and Janice Harper, eds., *The Women and International Development Annual.* Vol. 4. Boulder, Colo.: Westview Press.

Foley, Michael W., and Robert Edwards. 1996. "The Paradox of Civil Society." *Journal of Democracy* 7(3): 38-52.

Foster, James, and Amartya Sen. 1997. "On Economic Inequality after a Quarter Century." 2nd ed. Oxford: Clarendon Press.

Fox, Jonathan. 1993. *The Politics of Food in Mexico: State Power and Social Mobilisation.* Ithaca: Cornell University Press.

Galtung, Johan. 1994. *Human Rights in Another Key.* Cambridge, U.K.: Polity Press.

Gelles, Richard J., and Murray Straus 1998. *Intimate Violence.* New York: Simon and Schuster.

Giddens, Anthony. 1984. *The Constitution of Society.* Oxford: Blackwell.

Goetz, Anne Marie. 1998. "Women in Politics and Gender Equity on Policy: South Africa and Uganda." *Review of African Political Economy* 76: 241-62.

Greeley, Martin. 1994. "Measurement of Poverty and Poverty of Measurment." *IDS Bulletin 25*(2).

Grootaert, Christiaan. 1998. "Social Capital: The Missing Link?" Social Capital Initiative Working Paper No. 3. Social Development Family. Washington, D.C.: World Bank.

Grootaert, Christiaan. 1999. "Social Capital, Household Welfare, and Poverty in Indonesia." Policy Research Working Paper 2148. Social Development Family., Washington, D.C.: World Bank.

Grootaert, Christiaan, and Deepa Narayan. 1999. "Local Institutions, Poverty and Household Welfare in Bolivia." Social Development Family. Environmentally and Socially Sustainable Development Network. Washington, D.C.: World Bank.

Holland, Jeremy, and James Blackburn, eds., 1998. *Whose Voice? Participatory Research and Policy Change.* London: Intermediate Technology Publications.

Hyden, Goran. 1997. "Civil, Society, Social Capital, and Development: Dissection of a Complex Discourse." *Studies in Comparative International Development* 32: 3-30.

Jackson, Cecile. 1996. "Rescuing Gender from the Poverty Trap." *World Development* 23:489-504.

Jain, Devaki. 1996. "Panchayat Raj: Women Changing Governance." Gender in Development Programme. United Nations Development Programme, New York.

Kabeer, Naila. 1997. "Women, Wages and Intra-household Power Relations in Urban Bangladesh." *Development and Change* 28(2): 261-302.

Kabeer, Naila, and Ramya Subrahmanian. 1996. *Institutions, Relations and Outcomes: Framework and Tools for Gender-aware Planning.* University of Sussex; U.K.: Institute of Development Studies.

Kaufmann, Georgia. 1997. "Watching the Developers: A Partial Ethnography." In R.D. Grillo and R.L. Stirrat, eds., *Discourses of Development: Anthropological Perspectives.* Oxford: Berg Press.

Korten, David C. 1990. *Getting to the 21st Century: Voluntary Action and the Global Agenda.* West Hartford, Conn.: Kumarian Press.

Krishna, Anirudh, and Norman Uphoff. 1999. "Mapping and Measuring Social Capital: A Conceptual and Empirical Study of Collective Action for Conserving and Developing Watersheds in Rajasthan, India." Social Capital Initiative Working Paper No. 13. Washington, D.C.: World Bank.

Krishan, Anirudh, Norman Uphoff, and Milton J. Esman (eds.), 1997. *Reason for Hope: Instructive Experiences in Rural Development.* West Hartford, Conn.: Kumarian Press.

Leach, Melissa, Robin Mearns, and Ian Scoones. 1997. *Community-Based Sustainable Development: Consensus or Conflict?* University of Sussex, U.K.: Institute of Development Studies.

Lipton, Michael, and Martin Ravallion. 1995. "Poverty and Policy." In Jere Richard Behrman and Thirukodikaval Nilakanta Srinivasan, eds. *Handbook of Development Economics.* Vol. 3. Amsterdam: Elsevier Press.

MacEwen Scott, Alison. 1995. "Informal Sector or Female Sector? Gender Bias in Urban Labour Maket Models." In Diane Elson, ed., *Male Bias in the Development Process.* 2nd ed. Manchester, U.K.: Manchester University Press.

Marshall, Gordon. 1994. *The Concise Oxford Dictionary of Sociology.* New York: Oxford University Press.

Max-Neef, Manfred. 1993. *Human Scale Development: Conception, Application, and Further Reflections.* London: Apex Press.

Milanovic, Branko. 1998. *Income, Inequality, and Poverty During the Transition from Planned to Market Economy.* Regional and Sectoral Studies. Washington, D.C.: World Bank.

Milimo, John T. 1995. "An Analysis of Qualitative Information on Agriculture: from Beneficiary Assessments, Participatory Poverty Assessments and Other Studies which used Qualitative Research Methods." Ministry of Agriculture, Food, and Fisheries. Lusaka, Zambia.

Moore, Mick, and James Putzel. "Thinking Strategically about Politics and Poverty." IDS Working Paper 101. University of Sussex, U.K.: Institute of Development Studies.

Moser, Caroline. 1998. *The Asset-Vulnerability Framework: Reassessing Urban Poverty Reduction Strategies.* Washington, D.C.: World Bank.

Moser, Caroline, Annika Tornqvist, and Bernice van Bronkhorst. 1998. "Mainstreaming Gender and Development in the World Bank: Progess and Recommendations." Washington, D.C.: World Bank.

Narayan, Deepa. 1999. "Bonds and Bridges: Social Capital and Poverty." Policy Research Working Paper 2167. Policy Research Department. Washington, D.C.: World Bank.

Narayan, Deepa, and Katrinka Ebbe. 1997. "Design of Social Funds: Participation, Demand Orientation, and Local Organisational Capacity." Discussion Paper No. 375. Washington, D.C.: World Bank.

Narayan, Deepa, and Lant Pritchett. 1999. "Cents and Sociability: Household Income and Social Capital in Rual Tanzania." *Economic Development and Cultural Change* (47)4: 871-878.

Narayan, Deepa, and Lyra Srinivasan. 1994. *Participatory Development Tool Kit: Training Materials for Agencies and Communities* Washington, D.C.: World Bank.

Narayan, Deepa and Michael Cassidy. 1999. "A Dimensional Approach to Measuring Social Capital: Development and Validation of a Social Capital Inventory." Draft. Washington, D.C.: World Bank.

Narayan, Deepa, and Talat Shah. 2000. *Gender Inequity, Poverty, and Social Capital.* Policy Research Report on Gender Development, Working Paper Series. Washington, D.C.: World Bank.

North, Douglas. 1990. "Institutions and their Consequences for Economic Performance." In Karen Schweers Cook and Margaret Levi, eds., *The Limits of Rationality*. Chicago, Ill.: University of Chicago.

Norton Andy, and Thomas Stephens. 1995. "Participation in Poverty Assessments." Social Development Papers 9. Washington, D.C.: World Bank.

Orbach, Susie. 1999. "Psycho Analysis and Social Policy." Seminar Paper Presented to the World Bank, Washington, D.C.: April.

Patton, Michael Quinn. 1990. *Qualitative Evaluation and Research Methods*. Newbury Park, Calif.: Sage Publications.

Portes, Alejandro. 1998. "Social Capital: Its Origins and Applications in Modern Sociology." *Annual Review of Sociology* 22: 1-24.

Pottier, Johan. 1997. "Towards an Ethnography of Participatory Appriasal and Research." In R.D. Grillo and R.L. Stirrat, eds., *Discourses of Development: Anthropological Perspectives*. Oxford, U.K.: Berg Press.

Putnam Robert, Robert Leonardi, and Raffaella Y. Nanetti. 1993. *Making Democracy Work: Civic Traditions in Modern Italy*. Princeton, N.J.: Princeton University Press.

Ravallion, Martin. 1995. "China's Lagging Poor Areas." *American Economic Review, Papers and Procedures* 89: 301-5.

Ray, Raka, and Anna Kortweg. 1999. "Women's Movements in the Third World: Identity, Mobilisation and Autonomy." *Annual Review of Sociology* 25: 47-71.

Rietbergen-McCracken, Jennifer, and Deepa Narayan. 1998. "Participatory Tools and Techniques: A Resource Kit for Participation and Social Assessment" Social Policy and Resettlement Division, Environment Department. Washington, D.C.: World Bank.

Robb, Caroline. 1999. "Can the Poor Influence Poverty? Participatory Poverty Assessments in the Developing World." Washington, D.C.: World Bank.

Rodrik, Dani. 1998. "Globalisation, Social Conflict and Economic Growth." *World Economy* 21(1): 43-58.

Rupesinghe, Kumar, and Marcial Rubio. 1994 *The Culture of Violence.* New York: United Nations University Press.

Salmen, Lawrence. 1987. *Listen to the People.* New York; Oxford University Press.

Salmen, Lawrence. 1995. "Participatory Poverty Assessment: Incorporating Poor People's Perspectives into Poverty Assessment Work." Social Development Paper No. 11. Washington, D.C.: World Bank.

Salmen, Lawrence. 1998. "Toward a Listening Bank: A Review of Best Practices and the Efficacy of Beneficiary Assessment." Social Development Paper No. 23. Washington, D.C.: World Bank.

Sartori, Giovanni. 1997. "Understanding Pluralism." *Journal of Democracy* 8(4): 58-69.

Schuler, Sidney Ruth, Syed M. Hashemi, and Shamsul Huda Badal. 1998. "Men's Violence Against Women in Rural Bangladesh: Undermined or Exacerbated by Microcredit Programmes?" *Development in Practice* 8(2): 148-57.

Schwartz, S.H. 1994. "Are There Universal Aspects in the Structure and Contents of Human Values?" *Journal of Social Issues* 50(4): 19-45.

Sen, Amartya K. 1981. *Poverty and Famines.* Oxford: Clarendon Press.

Sen, Amartya K. 1983. "Poor, Relatively Speaking." *Oxford Economic Papers* 35: 153-69. Reprinted in *Resources, Values and Development.*

Sen, Amartya K. 1984. "Rights and Capabilities." In Amartya K. Sen, ed., *Resources, Values and Development.* Oxford, U.K.: Blackwell.

Sen, Amartya K. 1985. "A Sociological Approach to the Measurement of Poverty: A Reply to Professor Peter Townsend." *Oxford Economic Papers* 37: 669-76.

Sen, Amartya K. 1992. *Inequality Reexamined.* Cambridge, Mass: Harvard University Press.

Sen, Amartya K. 1993. "Economic Regress: Concepts and Features." *Proceedings of the World Bank Annual Conference on Development Economics,* 315-54.

Sen, Amartya K. 1997. *On Economic Inequality.* 2nd ed. Oxford: Clarendon Press.

Sen, Amartya K. 1999. *Development as Freedom.* New York: Knopf Press.

Shah, Shekhar. 1999. "Coping with Natural Disasters: The 1998 Floods in Bangladesh." Seminar Paper Presented in June to the World Bank, Washington, D.C.

Shapiro, Gilbert, and John Markoff. 1997. "A Matter of Definition." In Carl W. Roberts, ed., *Text Analysis for the Social Sciences.* Mahwah, N.J.: Lawrence Erlbaum Assoicates.

Silverman, David. 1993. *Interpreting Qualitative Data: Methods for Analyzing Talk, Text and Interaction.* Thousand Oaks, Calif.: Sage Publications.

Srinivas, Smita. 1999. *Social Protection for Women Workers in the Informal Economy.* Draft. Washington, D.C.: World Bank and Geneva; International Labour Office.

Standing, Guy. 1999. "Global Feminisation Through Flexible Labour: A Theme Revisited." *World Development* 3(27): 583-602.

Stone, P.J., D.C. Dunphy, M.S. Smith, and D.M. Ogilvie. 1966. *The General Inquirer: A Computer Approach to Content Analysis.* Cambridge: MIT Press.

Strauss, Anselm. 1987. *Qualitative Analysis for Social Scientists.* New York: Cambridge University Press.

Tarrow, Sidney. 1994. *Power in Movement: Social Movements, Collective Action and Politics.* Cambridge, U.K.: Cambridge University Press.

Tendler, Judith. 1997. *Good Government in the Tropics. Baltimore,* Md.: Johns Hopkins University Press.

Townsend, Peter. 1971. *The Concept of Poverty.* London: Heinemann Educational.

Tripp, Aili Mari. 1992. "The Impact of Crisis and Economic Reform on Women in Urban Tanzania." In Lourdes Benerla and Shelly Feldman (eds.), *Unequal Burden: Economic Crises, Persistent Poverty, and Women's Work.* Boulder, Colo.: Westview Press.

Uphoff, Norman. 1986. *Local Institutional Development: An Analytical Source Book with Cases.* West Hartford, Conn.: Kumarian Press.

Uphoff, Norman, Milton J. Esman, and Anirudh Krishna. 1997. *Reasons for Success: Learning from Instructive Experiences in Rural Development.* West Hartford, Conn.: Kumarian Press.

Visaria, Leela. 1999. "Violence Against Women in India: Evidence from Rural Gujarat." In *Domestic Violence in India: A Summary Report of Three Studies.* Washington, D.C.: International Center for Research on Women.

Weber, Robert Philip. 1990. *Basic Content Analysis.* 2nd ed. Newbury Park, Calif.: Sage Publications.

WHO (World Health Organisation). 1997. *Violence Against Women.* Geneva.

Woolcock, Michael. 1998. "Social Capital and Economic Development: Toward a Theoretical Synthesis and Policy Framework." *Theory and Society* 27(2): 151-208.

Woolcock, Michael, and Deepa Narayan. 2000. "Social Capital: Implications for Development Theory, Research, and Policy." *World Bank Research Observer* 15(2), Washington, D.C.: World Bank.

World Bank. 1996a. *From Plan to Market: World Development Report 1996.* Washington, D.C.

World Bank. 1996b. *Source Book on Participation.* Washington, D.C.

World Bank. 1997a. *Poverty Assessment: A Process Review*. Operations Evaluation Department Document 15881. Washington, D.C.

World Bank. 1997b. *World Development Report 1997: The State in a Changing World*. New York: Oxford University Press (for the World Bank).

World Bank. 1998. *World Development Indicators*. Washington, D.C.

World Bank. 1999. *World Development Indicators*. Washington, D.C.

World Bank. 2000. *Poverty Trends and Voices of the Poor*. Poverty Reduction Group. Washington, D.C.

Wratten, Ellen, 1995. "Conceptualizing Urban Poverty." *Environment and Urbanisation* 7: 11-36.

❑ ❑ ❑

Index